BASIC HANDBOOK OF POLICE SUPERVISION

BASIC HANDBOOK OF POLICE SUPERVISION

A Practical Guide for Law Enforcement Supervisors

By

GERALD W. GARNER

Chief of Police
Greeley Police Department
Greeley, Colorado

CHARLES C THOMAS • PUBLISHER, LTD.
Springfield • Illinois • U.S.A.

Published and Distributed Throughout the World by

CHARLES C THOMAS • PUBLISHER, LTD.
2600 South First Street
Springfield, Illinois 62704

© 2014 by CHARLES C THOMAS • PUBLISHER, LTD.

ISBN 978-0-398-08760-9 (paper)
ISBN 978-0-398-08782-1 (ebook)

Library of Congress Catalog Card Number: 2013041365

With THOMAS BOOKS *careful attention is given to all details of manufacturing
and design. It is the Publisher's desire to present books that are satisfactory as to their
physical qualities and artistic possibilities and appropriate for their particular use.*
THOMAS BOOKS *will be true to those laws of quality that assure a good name
and good will.*

Printed in the United States of America
SM-R-3

Library of Congress Cataloging-in-Publication Data

Garner, Gerald W.
  Basic handbook of police supervision : a practical guide for law enforcement
supervisors / by Gerald W. Garner, Chief of Police, Greeley Police Depart-
ment, Greeley, Colorado.
      pages cm
  Includes index.
  ISBN 978-0-398-08760-9 (pbk.) -- ISBN 978-0-398-08782-1 (ebook)
  1. Police--Supervision of--Handbooks, manuals, etc. 2. Police administration-
-Handbooks, manuals, etc. 3. Law enforcement--Handbooks, manuals, etc. I.
Title.

  HV7936.S8G358 2014
  363.2'2--dc23

                                                                    2013041365

To Kathy

PREFACE

At one time or another in his or her career, every law enforcement supervisor has wished for a handbook providing reliable guidance on what to do next. For most supervisors, that moment of wishful thinking comes many times over a leadership career.

This is that handbook. Written by a veteran law enforcement leader and compiled from the experiences, both good and bad, of a lot of law enforcement supervisors, it offers practical, no-frills advice about what to do to counter the day-to-day challenges and outright calamities that make up the first-line leader's work life. Perhaps even more important, it offers time-proven recommendations on how to prevent a bothersome situation from escalating into crisis proportions in the first place.

The handbook will prove equally useful to the veteran, novice, or future law enforcement supervisor. Its sound advice will help him retain his emotional as well as physical and moral health in a real-world environment that seems to become more challenging every day. It will help him to lead and bring his people to share his practices and beliefs in doing a very critical job the *right* way.

Just as it should be, the handbook is short on theory and long on "how to" advice. It is literally a resource that the supervisor can tuck into an equipment bag, or otherwise keep close at hand. It will help him grasp his difficult job's various demands, balance competing interests and excel as a leader, all the while serving as an exceptional role model for his employees. It likewise will aid him in carrying out the very practical tasks of communicating effectively, evaluating employee performance, correcting inappropriate behavior and helping his officers survive both on the street and in the police organization. Meanwhile, the handbook will assist the law enforcement leader in working well with his own boss and planning his own career.

There is no job description in the world quite like that of first-line law enforcement boss. The job is as unique as it is difficult and vital to the success of any successful police organization. Fortunately, the position is generally staffed by extremely competent people with organizational as well as physical courage. This book will help them become even better at their very important job.

G.W.G.

INTRODUCTION

The law enforcement supervisor faced with the challenges of the street is really not looking for philosophical discussions of the finer points of leadership and personnel management theory. Rather, he most often needs practical advice for solving the real-life problems he faces on the job each day. That is precisely the kind of "how to" advice this handbook provides.

The handbook combines the lessons of the author's 43-year law enforcement career with the actual experiences of a lot of first-line police leaders. Some of these lessons have been learned the hard way. The purpose of the book is to impart the knowledge without sharing the pain another law enforcement leader may have experienced in the process of gaining the information. Most of the challenges faced by today's law enforcement supervisors have been confronted (and solved) before. The actors and the stage may have changed; the script is often the same.

Chapter 1 will help the supervisor understand his new role now that he's not "one of the guys" anymore. Chapter 2 examines the leader's many obligations while the book's third chapter seeks to help the supervisor balance his host of new tasks.

Being a positive role model is one of the first-line leader's most important jobs, and Chapter 4 will help him in his quest to serve as an exceptional model for his employees to emulate. Chapter 5 will help him fill his leadership toolbox while Chapter 6 provides time-proven guidelines for communicating effectively – an absolute must if he is to excel as a leader. Meanwhile, Chapter 7 will help the supervisor master one of his toughest tasks: measuring the performance of his subordinates.

Chapter 8 will aid the supervisor in receiving and investigating complaints of employee misconduct. Chapter 9 provides practical advice in administering corrective action to his personnel. The chapter will not teach him to enjoy handing out discipline. Instead, it will help him fix broken behavior and save careers. Chapter 10 provides him with the basics for keeping those same employees safe in the face of the many dangers of the law enforcement officer's job.

On occasion, the front-line supervisor will find himself confronted on-scene by the ladies and gentlemen of the news media. Chapter 11 tells him how to feed the newshounds without getting bitten. In Chapter 12, the police boss will learn the organizational survival tricks of the trade for surviving his own boss, while Chapter 13 will help guide him safely through the minefields of his own organization with its always present politics and pitfalls.

Chapter 14 will guide the law enforcement supervisor in gathering all he has learned about leadership into building a successful career for himself. The book's next and final chapter offers practical advice for the leader deciding where to take his next career step.

This basic handbook is indeed a practical guide for today's law enforcement supervisor. Coupling that knowledge with his own good judgment and common sense, he should be well-prepared for whatever challenges the future might bring.

CONTENTS

BASIC HANDBOOK OF POLICE SUPERVISION

Chapter 1

HOW TO MASTER YOUR ROLE

You gained a lot when you became a supervisor. You certainly gained a lot of additional responsibilities. You gained additional respect and prestige, too. You doubtlessly began receiving a bit fatter paycheck and may have picked up some additional perks, as well. Hopefully, your gains were substantial once you sewed on those brand new stripes.

But you gave up some things when you became a supervisor, too. For one thing, you gave up the questionable privilege of griping about anything and everything concerning your organization and its leaders in front of whatever audience you might choose, whether inside or outside the department. You surrendered the option of damning the chief, the captain and your own immediate supervisor in front of your former colleagues who are now your subordinates. You gave up the ability to yammer about problems without proffering a realistic solution. ("Shoot the whole bunch" is not a realistic solution.)

You gave up a lot, alright. But you did not give up anything that an ethical and competent leader requires to do his job, and do it well. In this case, the major change that has occurred in your work life will be a good thing. Your bosses certainly thought you were capable of mastering change, or they would not have chosen you for the role of supervisor in the first place.

Change for the better is still change, however, and change frequently does not occur without emotional fallout. Even good change can bring psychological upset. That's the topic to be explored next.

YOU'RE NOT ONE OF THE GUYS ANYMORE

You may have noticed it even before you affixed those new chevrons to your uniform shirt. While they were still friendly enough, your old pals just didn't treat you exactly the same as they did before. They may not have seemed quite as chummy, quite as unguarded in what they said in front of you. Your shift from buddy to boss had begun. You likely felt the change, however minor. To many of your friends, you were now one of *them*: the brass.

If it is any comfort to you, the "change" occurs in every kind of work, from the oil field to the battle field to the board room. Former peers are at least a little uneasy hanging and interacting with old acquaintances who are now their bosses. How great or how minor the discomfort for everyone involved depends upon a lot of things, ranging from the nature of the former relationship to the personalities of the individuals themselves. Whatever the case, the discomfort is often very real.

You almost certainly thought about the reality that former relationships would change before you ever decided to go for promotion. You already determined that you could handle the potential downsides in exchange for the benefits that your new role would bring. If not, you must face that truth now. Fortunately, if you are anything like the vast majority of your law enforcement peers who made the jump successfully you will determine that the favorable consequences of promotion greatly outnumber the bad.

Even more good news for you is that you do not have to stop associating with your old work pals. You can still have a beer with them or take in the big game. You simply have to handle yourself just a little differently in their presence. You might say that you have a new outlook.

A NEW OUTLOOK

Now that you are the boss, you are expected to see a few things differently than you did as a first-line officer. For one thing, you are expected to take in the bigger picture of your organization that extends well beyond yourself, your assignment, your unit. As a patrol officer you had to concentrate on doing your own job well. What was going on in other parts of the agency may not have concerned you a great deal, so long as those doings were not obviously impacting you directly. You may not have much cared if the detectives were getting their fair share of resources or not so long as you were getting yours. Your own requirements were, after all, priority number one.

As a supervisor, you have to see the need for sharing resources agency-wide. Furthermore, you have to support filling that need through both words and action. On occasion that may mean offering personnel or other resources to another part of the department when you dearly would like to have them for yourself. That's called seeing the bigger picture that exists beyond your own slice of the larger pie that is a law enforcement organization. It is part of your new outlook on your work life.

Your revised outlook also has changed the way you look at some of those around you. Your line-level friends are now also your subordinates. In all likelihood, some of them are the people you must train, counsel, evaluate and lead. They are people you must, in a word, supervise.

At the same time, your superiors are no longer distant authority figures whom you can easily avoid. Now, some of them are your immediate bosses to whom you must turn for direction and advice. You are obligated to follow their orders. Indeed, things have changed in your world.

Your outlook likewise has been altered drastically in what you can ethically say to others about your peers and your supervisors. You undermine and weaken your fellow supervisors if you speak badly of them in front of your subordinates. You cause them equally serious damage if you permit your employees to say bad things about them in your presence. It matters not if you agree with what your troops are saying. Permitting attacks on your colleagues in your presence is intensely disloyal and destructive to the organization in which you have been promoted to the position of leader.

This same prohibition on public criticism (or the tolerance of it) holds true when the individuals under attack occupy the upper echelons of your department. Once more, only bad things (including decreased respect for you from your subordinates) can result from the tolerance of such misbehavior. Your ethics as a leader do not permit such a morally lazy response. You are too good, too much of a leader for that.

Your very necessary change in outlook means that you look at the police organization much differently than you did as a front-line trooper. Your world has to be bigger now. Try to picture a supervisor, a leader in your organization whom you have always admired and perhaps wanted to emulate. How did he or she appear to view the organization? How did he or she look, sound and act in front of subordinates? The positive role modeling of that leader is what you are striving to duplicate. (More about role modeling later.)

A changed outlook does not mean less fun or freedom for you. Far from it. Sergeants tend to have more fun than anyone else in the department! An altered outlook does, however, call for a personal reassessment of what you can say and do in the presence of others. If you previously harbored the nasty habit of operating your mouth before engaging your brain, you will need to curtail the practice now. Your common sense not to mention your organizational survival requires no less.

Your new outlook is in no way a bad thing. It is what an effective leader masters and maintains. It is an integral part of the leader you have become.

WHAT YOU CAN (AND CAN'T) DO NOW

As noted, your world has changed in that you are faced with a new set of things you can and cannot do to add to the long list of other "rules" you follow as a law enforcement professional. These guidelines provide a framework for your job performance as a leader. They include the following:

- You CAN help influence the future direction of the agency. Believe it or not, the decisions you make or participate in today will help shape what your organization will look like in the future. That's one reason you want to always do your best and keep an eye cast on the future. The personnel you help guide and train today will be the department's future, even when you are no longer part of the organization.
- You CAN contribute to the effort to recruit and hire the best people. That's a huge part of building the agency's future. You should always be on the lookout for new "talent" and seek to attract good prospects to the organization. Their presence may help make your own job easier today. Tomorrow they will run the department once

you have moved on. A good leader cares about what happens when he is no longer part of the picture.

- You CAN ably represent your agency and your profession in the community. You know that you are part of a good organization serving a noble profession. But you will run into a lot of otherwise smart people who don't know that. What you say about your department and your profession can impact a lot of individuals. You should strive to leave a good impression on each one via your actions as well as your words. *Look* for the chance to talk about what you do.

- You CAN set a great example as a positive role model. It's what your subordinates need from you more than anything else. As a leader your job is to SHOW, not TELL them how an ethical, professional peace officer works and lives. There is a great deal they can learn from you. Make sure that all of it is something you can be proud of.

- You CAN coach and mentor young talent. Many of your rookies will look to you for guidance on how to pursue their law enforcement careers. Others won't ask, but require guidance all the same. Go out of your way to spend time with them. Find out what is on their minds and what concerns them. You can strengthen both them and the agency by helping these youngsters learn the same lessons you did – but perhaps minus some of the pain!

- You CAN learn your boss's job and prepare for advancement. If you are truly good at your job as a leader, the agency needs your skills and abilities in its upper echelons. Here is the opportunity to have even more influence on where the department is going through sound decision making. You get there by learning what your boss is doing so you can join (or replace) him or her one day. And there's nothing wrong with telling the boss what you're up to and asking his help as you learn. Leaders worthy of the name will be anxious to help you, just as you are willing to coach and mentor your own subordinates.

- You CAN further your education and professional training. It is important that you never stop learning, both in life and in your profession. Attend relevant classes, conferences and seminars when you can. Share what you learn with others. In so doing you'll be bettering the department at the same time you help yourself prepare for the future.

• You CAN provide invaluable connections between the top and bottom layers of your organization. Communication is the name of the game. Few organizations have sufficiently excellent information flow between the top level leaders and the workers in the trenches. By passing the word with accuracy in both directions you can make your own department's communication efforts more effective. Accuracy is, of course, the key. This is not the place for personal editorial comment or unnecessary filtering.

On the other hand:

• You CAN'T gripe about the department without offering realistic solutions. You gave up that dubious privilege when you became a supervisor. You can still vent your spleen, but the place to do it is not in front of your employees. When you do air your grievances, try to have a reasonable alternative to whatever is vexing you. Your own boss is much more likely to listen to you if you focus on how to make it better as opposed simply to cursing the status quo.

• You CAN'T criticize the brass to your troops. You gave that one up when you became a leader, as well. You want (and need) your people to admire you. They won't, even if they claim to share your sentiments in front of you, if you tear down your organization's leadership. Once again, do your griping in private. Your people should see that your loyalty to the organization includes loyalty to its leadership unless and until that leadership proves truly dishonest or unethical.

• You CAN'T undermine your fellow supervisors. You may not like or admire or even trust one of your fellow supervisors. That happens on occasion in virtually all organizations. If that is the case for you, you obviously should carefully monitor all of your dealings with that individual. At the same time, you cannot share your ill feelings with your subordinates. Doing so undermines the unity of purpose that must govern the relations between all supervisors of the organization. If you must, discuss your beef with your contrary peer. Maybe you can work it out, or bring it up to your own boss, but do not air your negative feelings in the presence of your charges.

• You CAN'T set bad examples in your work or personal life. It's not enough to tell your people what to do. You must show them, too. That's one of their best avenues for learning. You want your people vowing that they want to be like you one day. You have betrayed your profession and your own ethics if the example you leave for them to follow is a bad one.

- You CAN'T display a "bad attitude." It's been said before in slightly different ways but it is important enough to bear repeating. Even when you're feeling bad, abused, unhappy and depressed you still need to do your best to keep it out of the view (or hearing) of your troops. Yes, you're human and can have a bad day, or a whole series of them. But your funk should not infect those who follow you. Try, really try, to keep your temporary unhappiness out of their reach. Remember that they are eternally watching and taking their cues from your behavior.
- You CAN'T fail to do your best. It's likely that your personality already demands that you do a lot, perhaps even more than you should, even on those rare days when you don't feel like it. Once again, your people are observing you. Since you don't want them putting in a half-hearted effort, you cannot afford to, either. Stay home if you're sick. Call on a peer to fill in for you if you're not up to the current challenge, whatever the reason. But don't sleepwalk your way through your job, not ever. Too much is riding on what you do.
- You CAN'T break the rules. It's part of that role modeling thing, yet again. Where your ethics are concerned, bad means never justify good ends. Don't cheat. Don't cut corners. Don't make excuses for bad behavior. Show your people the importance of following the rules by doing it yourself, from the way you fill out your time card to the way you treat a mouthy drunk to the way you interact with your family.
- You CAN'T choose sides and participate in intradepartmental fights and intrigue. Organizational politics, power plays and related skullduggery are, unfortunately, part of the DNA of most organizations, cop ones included. The temptation to indulge yourself in the game-playing can be great, particularly if the prospect of self-gain is being dangled in one form or another. Ethics should tell you to stay clear. If not, think about this tip on organizational survival: one side or the other generally loses. You may be on the "losing" side. Things could get unpleasant for the losers. You can't be bitten by the shark if you stay out of the water. If you've paid attention to what you've read so far, you *should* have better things to do.

All of that amounts to a lot to think about. Still, you are going to do a lot of thinking as a law enforcement supervisor. Knowing that you will follow this list of what to do and not do is probably a reasonable expectation by your own supervisor. Chances are, from observing your past behavior he or she already knows that you are absolutely capable of getting it done.

GUIDELINES TO LIVE BY

Every line of work has its rules and guidelines. Law enforcement has more than its share. Almost certainly your organization has a fat collection of orders, policies, procedures and regulations. If you are to be an effective supervisor, you must know what's in the rule book and be able to discern the details of an obscure regulation in short order. That's part of your job.

But there is another group of guidelines you need to be aware of as a well-rounded and competent leader. These are the so-called "rules to live by" for good supervisors. The list can vary a little from one police organization to the next. Nevertheless, regardless of the locale there remains a core set of guidelines that you will be well-served to learn. The list includes the following:

Seek respect, not affection. No matter how great a person you are, no matter how competent your performance as a law enforcement supervisor, not everyone will like you. It's even possible that a few will outright despise you and wish bad things to befall you. That's something you expect when you deal with crooks. It's harder to take when you realize that on occasion a subordinate will feel that way, too. But it can happen. Whether based on a real or imaginary injustice that the individual feels he has suffered at your hands, he now dislikes you, perhaps intensely.

The standard reaction from a normal human being is to wonder what in the world he has done to earn such ill will. The feeling is normal, but you would be foolish to let it consume you with worry or puzzlement. Try to realize that it just happens sometimes and go on with your life. It is not your job to fix all unhappiness or ill will. It may be beyond fixing, anyway. Just determine that you always will treat others, including your subordinates, with fairness. Determine to continue to be an honest, decent human being. That much you owe to your subordinates, your organization and yourself. Strive to be as content as possible and go forward.

It is a fact of life that not everyone will love you. That's alright. It is their respect that you are seeking. That comes from knowing and doing your job well. It comes from treating all of your subordinates the same – fairly and with respect. That includes the ones that you don't particularly like and the ones you suspect don't like you. If in the process some of your people do like you a lot (and they will), consider that a bonus. But always be willing to settle for respect. It's enough. It will take you a long way down the road to a successful and contributing leadership career.

Make your expectations clear. It's not fair to expect your employees to read your mind. You will need to carefully and clearly spell out what it is you expect them to do. Ask if they have questions about what it is you are wanting. Be prepared to repeat yourself, as not everyone gets it the first time. It is also acceptable to ask questions of them yourself to be sure that they know what is expected, and within what time frame. In most cases, you'll probably want to leave as little as possible open to interpretation. Be concrete.

At the same time, keep in mind that you generally get not what you expect but what you inspect. Checking up is necessary. You can check without being a micromanager or snooper. Just keep your "checking" as informal and nonthreatening as possible. Your checkup visits should not look or feel like a standup inspection.

Realize that you can't be everything for everyone. You could make yourself crazy trying to do that. You are unlikely to succeed, anyhow. Just do your best to stay honestly interested in all of your people and treat each one with fairness. But you cannot fix every single thing that anyone ever complains about, nor should you try. Frankly, some people just like to gripe. If you remove one source of whining for them today, they will have replaced it with a new one by tomorrow. Seek to address legitimate problems. But know that not all of them are.

Respond on some calls, but stay out of the way. Your subordinates will expect to see you on-scene from time to time, but they won't appreciate it if your only purpose in being there is to create extra work for them. In other words, you are not a patrolman anymore. The patrol guys won't like it if you make finding drunks and traffic violators for them to handle a regular staple of your wandering the street. Just show up on occasion, demonstrate your interest and stay out of the way unless the officers clearly need (or ask for) your assistance.

The same advice holds true if you happen to be supervising detectives or other special assignment officers. Go to their scenes on occasion, but generally leave the handling of the assignment to them unless they obviously need your help. Your goal is to demonstrate your interest in what your people are doing without becoming a micromanager.

Take time to listen. There is no doubt that you are going to be busy as a supervisor. All the same, it's important that you always make time available for an employee who wants to talk to you. The subject matter may be earth-shaking or far from it. Regardless, you owe it to your subordinates to lend an ear when they need to talk. Every good supervisor is also a good listener. Sometimes that may require you to display some excellent acting skills when the topic your employee wants to talk about is not really of great interest to you. However, listening is always worth the energy you must put into it. What you learn may turn out to have considerable impact on your relationship with your subordinate and his or her peers, not to mention the work product that all of you deliver.

Don't neglect the personal touches. Employees often remember little things, like the boss acknowledging their birthday or an addition to the family. The same holds true when your subordinate has lost someone dear or experienced serious injury or illness in the family. Just a word or two of inquiry from you may be remembered for a long time. While they may deny it, most cops also appreciate an e-mail, text, handwritten note or just a mention in passing about work well done. It serves as evidence that you know and care about what they are doing. As long as it is sincerely meant, such acknowledgment is *always* worth the little time and effort it takes.

Always serve as a positive role model. Every one of your employees should be able to look to you to ascertain what a competent law enforcement professional looks, sounds and acts like. There is no substitute for setting a positive example for your people in everything you do, on duty and off. That does not mean you can never make a mistake or have a bad day. But when you do mess up, you are obliged to acknowledge your error and fix it. That is, after all, what you would expect your people to do. You cannot expect your employees or your organization to be any better than you are. Failing to serve as a positive role model is a cardinal sin for a leader. Don't do it. Not ever.

Emphasize the importance of safety equipment and behavior.
Your people reasonably expect you as their supervisor to look out for
their welfare. Nowhere is this expectation more intense than in the area
of officer safety. They will expect you to help assure that they have the
equipment necessary to carry out their work as safely as possible. They
will expect you to advocate for them when rules, policies or procedures
related to officer survival are under discussion by management. And
they will expect you to speak up on their behalf when they have per-
formed their duties according to reasonable officer safety guidelines
and now find themselves under attack by a citizen or the department's
brass. At such a time they will want you to be their spokesperson and
defender all the way up to the Big Boss, if need be.

You should never let yourself be sucked into using "officer safety" as
an excuse to cover for actual wrongdoing of any kind. When your people have done it the right way, most likely the way *you* have taught
them, they need to be able to count on finding you in their corner.
Don't turn up missing.

Some of these guidelines you will find discussed elsewhere in this
book. A good example can be found in the stated need for great role
modeling. That repetition is not accidental. These "supervisor's rules to
live by" are that important. They pertain to any number of your responsibilities as a leader. Rely on them to help put together your own
leadership toolbox.

SUMMARY

The job of law enforcement supervisor is unlike any other on the
planet. It brings big challenges. But it also offers great rewards. The
move from front-line officer to first-line supervisor remains the biggest
leap in law enforcement leadership. Not everyone can make the jump
successfully. The changes are huge, and that includes a change in outlook. You are expected to master a new role.

Now that you are not one of the guys anymore you will be expected
to see things a little differently. In order to be a successful leader, you
will have to look, sound and act a bit differently, too. Certain things you
used to do you can't do anymore. There will be other things to do and
say, instead. Mastering all of that will help make you an effective supervisor, a great leader.

As a supervisor you will find new rules to live by in your work-related world. None of them are unreasonable. None of them are beyond the skills and abilities you already have displayed in spades as an effective law enforcement officer. You can do this. Probably, you already are.

Chapter 2

HOW TO GRASP YOUR JOB'S DEMANDS

So what, exactly, does a supervisor *do?* You already know the answer to that one. He does a lot of things, actually, ranging from the training to the counseling and correction he provides to his subordinates. He works hard to be fair and even harder to serve always as a positive role model. He evaluates performance, he engages in planning and he serves as a complaint and grievance processor for the public as well as his own people. Most of all, he LEADS.

Virtually everything you will do as a supervisor depends upon your ability to lead your subordinates. You will be expected to lead and guide them in good times and bad, in the relative comfort of the briefing room and in the crucible of the streets. You will be expected to lead people who like and respect you and those who do neither. The latter characters are to be found in virtually any organization, law enforcement agencies included. On occasion they will make your job challenging and your life "interesting."

Leadership demands loyalty, not so much to a person as to an organization, a profession, an ideal. In the process of demonstrating that loyalty you will discover, if you have not done so already, that you are pulled in a number of directions all at the same time by a widely diverse set of demands on your time and talent. Put another way, as a leader you serve a number of masters, all of them good and legitimate ones. Nevertheless, ably tending all of them requires more than a little effort. This chapter is intended to help you do that.

WHAT YOU OWE YOUR BOSS

What you want and need from your boss are probably the same things that he or she wants and needs from you:

- Loyalty
- Open and honest communication
- Integrity
- Your best

Loyalty calls for more than refraining from calling your supervisor a hog-nosed snake in front of the roll call briefing, although that's expected, too. Loyalty requires that you consistently support your boss's decisions in public but tell him in private when he is clearly headed down the wrong path. Loyalty means giving your boss your honest opinions when he asks you for them, even when you suspect that hearing them will not make him happy. That kind of loyalty calls for personal courage.

Loyalty requires that you keep your boss advised of "intelligence" regarding your own organization, including the current products of the rumor mill and the significant personnel issues that are the daily bread of any law enforcement organization. Your goal should be to keep your supervisor from being surprised by something *his* boss would have expected him to know about. You do not like surprises from your subordinates. It's a good bet that your boss doesn't, either.

Loyalty, of course, involves much more than keeping the boss informed and refraining from calling him names. What you are seeking is an atmosphere in which mutual trust allows you and your boss to work comfortably together. That kind of relationship begins with good communication.

Just as in your life away from the job, good communication frequently translates into honesty and openness with those with whom you most frequently interact. It starts with telling the truth, even though it may feel more comfortable at the time to tell something else. (That comfort will evaporate like a raindrop on sizzling pavement when the truth comes out.) Good communication also calls for removing the filters from what you say and hear. One common example of such a destructive filter can be found in your boss's "negative" reputation or your own past, difficult relationship with him. It is your job to put those distractions aside now. The present is what is most important.

Almost everyone has had a boss that did not communicate well. Indeed, he or she may have harbored a lot of other "issues," as well. If that is your present situation it surely won't make your communication task any easier. Regardless, it remains your responsibility to assure that your end of the information exchange is carried out. The task is too important not to be done well.

Naturally, your supervisor also has the right to expect honesty and integrity from you in all things. This may be the "easiest" part of all that's involved in your relationship with your boss. When everything you do is steeped in absolute integrity (as it should be if you aspire to lead in this profession) then carrying that personal trait over to your interactions with your boss should not be difficult. Remain mindful, however, that absolute integrity for a leader means more than not pinching a candy bar at the 7-Eleven burglary scene. It means always giving your boss your honest views and conducting yourself as an excellent role model in front of your subordinates and your community. Integrity is something you wear like a uniform. Make sure that yours fits you well.

You expect your boss always to give you his best, including his time and full attention whenever you need it. You expect him to support you fully, especially when things get dicey. He has the right to expect the same from you. Supervising law enforcement personnel is not a part-time job or an easy one, as you well know. It requires your full engagement to do it well. Don't be found wanting when your supervisor looks to you for support.

You always do your best on the street and in the trenches, regardless of your place in the organization. Your personal ethics would not permit you to do less. Be sure that you do the same in nurturing and maintaining the working relationship you have with your own supervisor and the leadership structure of which he is a part. By so doing you can be at your most effective in representing your subordinates' best interests as well as your own.

WHAT YOU OWE YOUR DEPARTMENT

In a word, your best. You have heard that before. Likely you have told your troops the same thing at one time or another. There may be no crying in baseball, but there can be no half-hearted efforts in law enforcement, either. Cops can get killed or hurt by sleepwalking their way through this job. You wouldn't permit it from your own people and you should expect that your employer won't accept less than your best from you. Give it your all.

Beyond your very best efforts you owe your employer a positive contribution to the image and reputation of the agency. You help build that reputation for good or ill by what you do in the community, on duty and off. Even if you do little more than be a good, law abiding citizen when you take off the uniform, you nevertheless support your department's good reputation by the life you lead. On the other hand, anything you do of a questionable or outright wrongful nature will be fixed on by the self-appointed law enforcement critics as one more example why the cops are not to be liked or trusted. You have just become ammunition in someone else's vendetta against law enforcement. And you may have just caused yourself problems that you'll have to explain to your boss very soon.

Additionally, you owe your organization your contributions as the consummate professional that you are. It is probable that your experience has brought you skills and knowledge that your agency needs badly. Whatever your area of specialized knowledge or expertise you should be willing to share it in strengthening your department. Don't be shy about sharing what you know and do well. In the process you will make your organization better.

WHAT YOU OWE YOUR SUBORDINATES

You owe them the same thing you owe your boss: your best. And what, exactly, does that mean? It means that you represent their views and needs to management while you communicate management's information and directions to them. It means you look out for your people's welfare without forgetting that you also look out for them by disciplining them when they go astray. Meanwhile, you assure that they are appropriately recognized for their good work. In other words, you lead.

In carrying out all of these responsibilities there are some specific tasks you must thoughtfully and successfully execute if you are to do your best for your subordinates. Those tasks include the following:

Set a great example. It's possible, even likely, that once upon a time you had a favorite supervisor you wanted to be like one day. It should be your goal to inspire your subordinates, or at least some of them, to want to follow in your footsteps someday. One way in which you accomplish that is by consistently doing your job and living your life in a manner that inspires both respect and admiration in your people. Your subordinates are watching your behavior, on duty and off. You want to be sure that the picture they get of you is a positive one. That means you must follow the rules and set a good example in both your professional and personal life Only then can you honestly expect the same of those copying you. All good leaders set good examples. That's why you will do the same at all times.

Tell the truth. There is really no acceptable substitute. Along with your integrity, your credibility – your believability – is among your most valuable attributes as a leader. Always telling the truth is part of the role modeling you do for your people as you go about setting a good example. As you know from life experience, lying may make things feel better at the moment but the falsehood generally comes back to bite you later on. Then you don't feel so good. You may even have made a bad situation a lot worse.

Everyone has told a well-intentioned lie, perhaps to help someone else feel better or save face. ("No, dear, of course that dress doesn't make you look fat.") The point is that even little lies, well-intentioned ones, can come back to haunt you when you are filling the shoes of a police supervisor. It's generally true that both your subordinates and your bosses need to get accurate information from you, even when that information might not serve to make them happy. They nevertheless deserve to hear the truth.

Avoid playing favorites. It sounds simple enough, yet the sin of favoritism is still committed by supervisors the world over. A fishing buddy gets a widely-sought special assignment. A pal avoids a detested task. An old friend obtains a leg up on a promotion denied to the rest of the team members. Favoritism by a leader breeds contempt among his subordinates. Rampant favoritism can even lead to the downfall of a supervisor. The solution is simple: resist the all-too-human temptation to engage in the practice of awarding special benefits to those you really like that are denied their equally-qualified peers. If your pal is really a pal, he'll understand.

At the same time, a friend or acquaintance should not be punished because of the relationship. He must not be treated worse than his compatriots just to permit you to make a point. As in everything else you do as a leader, equality and fairness should be your bywords.

Play fair. And speaking of fair, see to it that you always play by the rules that you rightfully would expect your people to follow. Leaders are not allowed to cheat, not ever. That requirement goes right along with the mandate not to lie. The role of supervisor is not the place to settle old grudges or punish new enemies. Treating police employee and citizen-customer alike with fairness, compassion and impartiality will help guarantee your reputation as a great leader who is to be admired and emulated.

Honestly represent your employees' views and interests. Here comes that requirement to tell the truth again, just slightly repackaged. You owe your employees your best effort at honestly representing their views and concerns to management. If they are complaining about an equipment issue or angry over a change in scheduling or deployment, the boss needs to hear that from you, absent filtering or varnishing of the truth. That does not mean that the boss needs to hear the employee's quote that "he's an idiot if he doesn't listen." You can accurately convey the urgency of the message without bringing down fire and brimstone on the head of the upset employee. But the boss does need to hear what is upsetting his people *before* the reaction goes critical.

Accurately relay leadership's directions. Management needs to have its directions accurately delivered to the personnel who will carry them out. The supervisor serves as an incredibly vital relay point in that communication process. The process is vital enough that it is mandatory that you ask questions and obtain clarifications if what is meant is unclear. Try to put yourself in your employees' places when they receive the word. Would *you* understand what was expected of you? This isn't the place to relay what you *guessed* was intended. You need to be sure. Neither is it the time to filter what was said in order to take the sting out of an assumed-unpopular order or decision. That mandate to always tell the truth is in play here, too.

Praise and correct, as appropriate. You've heard it before: praise in public, criticize in private. It is good advice and you should follow it in your interactions with your people. Never hesitate to praise good work; most people thrive on good words from a boss they admire. But be sure the praise is both merited and sincere; nothing falls flatter than a commendation issued just for breathing. Overdone praise loses its value for the recipient.

You also owe your people correction when they go off course. Correction should be direct but also in proportion for the error committed. In other words, you do not want to wield the proverbial sledgehammer to slay the proverbial fly. Your friends need correction as appropriate, too. It's for their good and that of the organization. You will know that you are too close to someone when you cannot hold them accountable for wrongdoing. Don't let that happen to you – it'll do neither of you any good.

Help them grow. Providing guidance and advice to his or her subordinates is something that every good supervisor does. On occasion it has to be done even when the subordinate really doesn't want to hear what the boss has to say. But constructive criticism, delivered at the right time and in the right place and leavened with some deserved praise, helps everyone get better. The supervisor owes that kind of guidance to his people.

Helping a subordinate grow also can mean steering him towards special training or a special assignment to further his career. Sometimes that training can be remedial in nature, sometimes it is intended to strengthen even more an already apparent aptitude for something. Helping your people grow even can include imposing discipline when a subordinate gets really off track. The goal of correction, of course, is always to encourage the resumption of good performance and a good career.

Really care. If you truly care about your people, their well-being and their professional development, they probably already know it. Most likely it shows. But most police people have pretty keen bullstuff detectors. Most can spot a phony a mile away. You don't want ever to fall into that category of despicable characters. It's absolutely necessary that you care, even when caring means making a wayward subordinate really unhappy by tugging his leash.

By looking out for your people and caring about what happens to them you are fulfilling one of your most vital duties as a leader. You are serving as a caretaker of your organization's future, as one or more of these people likely will replace you one day. The rookie trying hard to be invisible in the back row of your briefing room may be the chief of police when you have long since vacated the premises. You owe him, the department and the community the best you can do. Today you are helping shape the future. Honestly caring is where it starts.

WHAT YOU OWE YOUR PROFESSION

Over the years that you have been "in the business" you doubtlessly have heard a lot about what you owe your profession. It wasn't hype. Law enforcement truly is a "cause" that relatively few are called upon to share. It is something special, way above the 8 to 5 world of the average Joe or Sally. It demands a great deal, as you already have learned.

As a recognized leader in your law enforcement agency you will find yourself called upon for even more than the guy or gal who pushes a squad car or pounds a foot beat. As a supervisor you are expected to contribute to the profession, to help further its aims, ideals and image. There are a number of ways you can do this. You can teach, and share your knowledge and experience with those inside and outside your department. Some of your colleagues have done so in academy classrooms while others have instructed at the university or community college level.

You can write, too, either for one of the law enforcement trade publications or for internal consumption by your fellow employees. Almost without exception, law enforcement agencies need more qualified authors for training bulletins, procedural manuals and similar materials intended to help officers stay current in the ever-changing world of policing. The ability to write for clear understanding would appear to be a vanishing talent in today's world of abbreviated text messages. If you possess that ability, do not allow it to lie dormant. Your profession needs you.

You also support your profession by bettering it via your participation in professional groups and associations. Your contributions can come at the local, regional, state or national levels. You do not even have to take a leadership role in the group, although that's fine, too. It's certain that you can offer plenty through your active participation and support.

As you know all too well, the job you have chosen is not an eight to five weekdays proposition, especially for supervisors. Part of that beyond-forty-hours participation should be devoted to making your profession better through your personal involvement in it. At the same time you are doing that you are simultaneously bettering the community and the agency of which you are a member. But bolstering profession, organization and community does not come just from what you are doing. It comes from what you are *not* doing, too. By refraining from illegal, unethical, immoral or just plain *wrong* conduct both on duty and off you avoid harming your profession and its good image. "Old time" law enforcement resulted in enough black eyes, figuratively and literally. Today's much-improved profession doesn't need any fresh bruises. By setting a good example always you help build a professional reputation for yourself and your many thousands of colleagues.

You are a professional. You know that. Through continuous effort you can further the goals and the positive future of the noble profession of which you are a part.

WHAT YOU OWE YOURSELF

You can't take care of anyone else unless you first take care of yourself. You doubtlessly have heard that one before, too. It's true. There's a very good reason the flight attendant tells you to put on your own oxygen mask before you try to help anyone else.

Some of the elements involved in taking care of yourself are pretty obvious. You already know, or should, that taking care of yourself physically requires a good diet, consistent exercise program and overall healthy lifestyle. That healthy lifestyle does not include the drinking of alcohol to excess or the smoking of anything. It includes getting enough rest and sound sleep, too. It is your responsibility, not your employer's, to take care of yourself physically so that you can enjoy a long and fulfilling life. It's an added benefit that you'll also be safer and happier on the job.

You must not neglect your mental and emotional health, either. Your difficult job includes a good deal of stress, generated from both outside your organization and (worse) inside it. You need a healthy substitute for stress-generated worry, and for a lot of cops that means physical exercise. You also should not forget the advice you give your young officers, and never fail to practice it yourself: have somebody (or several somebodies) to whom you can talk openly about whatever is troubling you. It may be a close friend, spouse, or colleague. But there absolutely must be someone. You can pay back the favor by listening to that person in a noncritical manner. Both of you will be healthier for the experience. Talk it out.

Realize, too, that there may be times in which you will need to talk to a professional about something that is troubling you and just won't let go. There are plenty of excellent law enforcement psychologists and peer support specialists out there. Do not hesitate to avail yourself of the services of someone who is schooled to help you. You would not be "ashamed" to go to a doctor for a broken leg. There is no more reason to be hesitant to see someone who can help you address a brain-based malady.

Taking care of yourself includes strengthening your mind as well as your body. Your personal growth on and off duty should include life-long learning. Stretching your brain can be very self-satisfying in building your self-esteem. Putting some college credits to your name also can bolster your chances for advancing in your organization and profession. Most departments likewise encourage their leaders to continue their in-service education through attendance at specialized training courses. Take advantage of any reasonable opportunity offered for strengthening your resume. That's called career development and it's the name of the game for today's forward-looking law enforcement leader.

Finally, the intelligent law enforcement leader (that's you!) realizes that he best serves himself as well as his department, his people, his profession and his community when he acts as the ideal of what a law enforcement officer should be. That's all part of your personal ethical development, and it goes hand in hand with career development. By obeying the rules, on duty and off, he sets a good example for his troops and the public at large. By doing so he knows that he also can be justifiably proud of himself. By living his personal life in a moral way he denies those who would harm him and his agency the poison to do it with. You can do all of those things, and do them well.

You also take care of yourself when you show everyone by example what a "real cop" really is in the twenty-first century world. At a time when too many young people (including some of your subordinates) get their image of what a cop's life is all about from bad television shows and the gritty violence fests that pass for movies, your positive role modeling is more important than ever. A really good supervisor will see to it that the only image his troops and the public get of him is a positive one. It's doing the right thing for yourself, too.

SUMMARY

There is no more important job in law enforcement than that of first-line supervisor. Likely you already knew that. If he's as smart as he should be, your own boss certainly knows it, too. Assuredly the CEO of the outfit is also aware of the key role that you and your peers play in guiding the organization where it needs to go.

You respond to a lot of demands as a first-line leader. You owe your loyalty and your absolute best efforts to the chain of command that extends above you as well as to the employees who have been placed in your charge. That same loyalty and a pledge to do your best reach beyond to the entire organization of which you are a part. That debt extends even farther to the profession that you are proud to call your own.

In the process of taking care of your ethical obligations to others you must not overlook what you owe yourself. As in life in general, you cannot take care of others if you do not also take care of yourself. That obligation to self includes what you do for both your physical and emotional health. It includes what you do to better yourself as a person through your education, training and life itself. It includes what you do to assure that your work ethic and integrity are never found wanting.

It's important, alright, to grasp your job's demands. But never let your job's grasp on you become so tight that it restricts your ability to *enjoy* what you are doing in both your personal and professional life. You owe that to yourself and your loved ones.

Chapter 3

HOW TO BALANCE YOUR MANY TASKS

As a law enforcement leader you have a seemingly overwhelming list of duties and expectations placed on you by a host of "masters," ranging from your employees to your boss to your community. This lengthy roster of tasks can feel intimidating to the newly-minted supervisor who thought he would spend his work hours resolving tactical questions but instead found himself addressing employee grievances and citizen complaints far more often than overseeing crook-catching operations.

A healthy balance is what you are seeking in handling the many leadership tasks that come your way. Handling that balance must include keeping yourself physically and emotionally healthy. You help no one, especially you, if you allow yourself to be overwhelmed and overcome by the challenges of the job.

The good news for you is that bad things do not have to happen to good supervisors. It is by no means inevitable that you will be run over by the demands of the job. By applying your plentiful supply of good decision-making skills and plain old common sense you can balance your tasks and handle their challenges with both efficiency and effectiveness, all the while maintaining that comforting feeling of being in control and at the top of your game. The first step in balancing those tasks is knowing what they are.

YOUR ROLE AS A LEADER

A leader is an individual occupying a place or position in which he can influence the beliefs and actions of others. You are a leader in your organization and profession. You can do both of those things, and more.

You lead when you display commanding authority. That's what a good supervisor does, although the best ones play down the "commanding" part except when it must be brought to the fore, such as in the presence of a crisis in which there is no time or place for debate. An effective leader knows that authority is often best displayed in small doses. He or she follows the "Golden Rule" of leadership: treat others as you would wish to be treated – always.

There are a host of character and personality traits you will be expected to demonstrate as a good leader. Complete integrity is an absolute necessity. So is personal courage and loyalty to your organization and profession. You must be credible and believable. In other words, you must have an earned reputation for telling the truth. You must have the common sense that helps make you a good decision maker. You must be an exceptional motivator of other human beings. You additionally must be a great communicator who is capable of showing sincere empathy for his people and their plights.

As you will see and hear repeated time and time again, nothing is more important to your success as a leader than serving as a positive role model. You absolutely must set a good example. You will have to display the personal courage to lead even when you do not agree with the directions you have been given. You will be self-confident without crossing the line into arrogance. You will do your best to suppress rumors rather than helping spread them. You will not attack your boss or your organization in front of your subordinates. You will tell the truth, even when it hurts or makes your job harder, at least for the moment. You will set very high standards for yourself, including one for personal integrity. You will avoid holding grudges or showing favoritism, as you are only too aware that doing either is not a true leader's way.

As a leader you will have to connect with the community as well as your employees. If given the opportunity by your bosses, you will help establish the organization's mission, vision and values. You may be a subject matter expert in some technical or other aspect of your job. You will be an advocate for your agency out in the community and, perhaps, in front of the news media. You will defend your department, as required, and patiently explain, as needed, when people "just don't get it."

You will have yet other duties, as well. When an emergency or other situation dictates, you will still need to be able to perform as a frontline cop. You will serve as a sort of risk manager in helping to keep your people safe. (Much more about that later.) You will evaluate the performance of your people and correct and discipline them when necessary. You will work as a coach and mentor of your employees. You will help to recruit new talent to your organization. You will receive and resolve questions and complaints concerning why your people did what they did. You will, in a few words, labor always to leave the place better than you found it.

You also have at least one more important duty as a leader. You must do your part in the training of your people.

YOUR ROLE AS A TRAINER

As a leader, you are obligated to both your employees and your organization to help assure that your charges are adequately prepared to carry out their difficult and important jobs. Your task begins with determining what they need to assure their safety and effectiveness, both as individuals and as a team.

You will need to evaluate your employees as to their current degree of preparation for the job at hand. In other words, do they already possess the knowledge and skills to do their jobs well and do them safely? If any or all of them are lacking, it will be up to you to get them the training they need to overcome the problem. Every one of them may have different needs. You can bring at least some of the picture into focus by observing their performance. But do not overlook one of the most valuable tools in your possession for determining what's needed: *ask* them in a nonthreatening, noncritical manner. Then set out to obtain what is needed, whether it is training for an individual or a whole team. It is their responsibility to learn. But it is yours to help make the learning opportunity available.

Comprehensive officer safety training must be a part of every officer's personal "curriculum." But there's plenty more to be learned, too. The job of today's law enforcement officer is more complex than ever. Your people undoubtedly need to know more than you did when you came on the job. They may have to master technical skills that weren't even thought of when you became a cop. Their people skills must not be found wanting, either.

Beyond that, individual employees may need to acquire additional skills to help them fulfill their particular career plans. Find out what it is that they want to achieve. For one officer it may be promotion; for another it may be a tour in the detective bureau. Whatever the case, you can assist by pointing them in the direction of the needed experience, training or formal education and then leaving the rest up to them. You can counsel and suggest, recommend and encourage. You can advocate with the brass for the rather expensive school that will take an employee out of the duty lineup for a while. Beyond that, it's up to your prospective student to get the appropriate rear end in the right classroom chair.

As a part of your training duties you will need to determine where you can handle needed training yourself and where you will need to rely on others. You may be able to provide terrific guidance to fix an officer's report writing weaknesses but need help in the area of arrest control tactics. You cannot be an expert in every single area of law enforcement skills. Do not hesitate to call on others for help, just as they should be able to call on you.

Finally, you will need to assess whether or not the lessons of training have been learned. You might rely on a written test to see if the knowledge imparted in a roll call training classroom was learned. On the other hand, simply observing an officer's performance on the job may tell you if another specific skill was mastered and remembered. Further effort will be required if the new knowledge failed to take hold. The police officer's job is too critical and potentially too dangerous to be attempted without an adequate mastery of the requisite knowledge, skills and abilities. Helping to fill that gap, where it is found to exist, is where the responsible leader comes in.

YOUR ROLE AS A COUNSELOR

One of the most valuable (and sometimes the most painfully-learned) of the lessons mastered by a new supervisor is this one: your employees' problems are not your own. Do not attempt to own them.

There is nothing cold or uncaring in that logic. It simply means that while it is indeed your job to help your people get through their difficulties, on duty and off, in the end the solution of their problems remains their ultimate responsibility, not yours. As much as you may want to help, and *can* help, it will be up to the employee himself to solve his own difficulties. They are not yours.

As every veteran supervisor knows, the variety of tight spots a police employee can get himself or herself into is virtually limitless. The difficulties can include marital problems, financial reverses, ethical lapses, mental issues, actual criminal behavior and any combination of the preceding roster of troubles. One veteran of over forty years in the policing business put it this way: "These kids today haven't thought of any new ways to get themselves into trouble. They just have additional tools to do it with."

He was referring, of course, to the cell phones, e-mails, texting and hand-camera devices that are part and parcel of the twentieth-first century police person's toy bag. He knew from experience that poor judgment, misdirected and overzealous hormones and out-of-control egos are today still felling more than their share of law enforcement officers, young and old. He also recognized that many of the problems thus created will eventually be brought to the attention of the first-line leader.

As a leader you naturally want to help your people survive the problems that they have created for themselves as well as those that have been visited upon them through no fault of their own. It is the right and humane thing for you to do. It is also the right and practical thing for you to do so that your organization does not lose the investment it has put into an individual who may be in danger of leaving the profession, or at least ceasing to shoulder his share of the workload. In that case, your intervention would appear to be as needed for humane purposes as it is ethically required.

Addressing an employee problem, of course, requires recognizing that one exists in the first place. Of all the leaders in the organization, the first-line supervisor is the best placed to spot trouble in its earliest stages. If he knows his people as well as he should, he will suspect that something "just isn't right" and inquire further. The symptoms of problems brewed or brewing can be practically endless, but may include at least the following:

- Unexplained, excessive sick leave
- Increased number of citizen complaints

- Increased number of instances of use of force
- Employee appearing sleepy or distracted at work
- Major change in personality, such as a normally outgoing individual becoming withdrawn
- Chronic disagreements with co-workers
- Regular tardiness to work
- Increasing workplace accidents involving the employee
- Multiple lawsuits or "intent to sue" notices involving the employee
- Unusual or outright bizarre behavior
- Employee involved in incidents of alleged workplace violence or harassment
- Drastic slide in quality and/or quantity of work produced
- Employee appears under the influence of alcohol or drugs
- Evidence (such as empty containers) of alcohol or drug abuse
- Marked deterioration in grooming or uniform/clothing appearance
- Newly-developed "attitude" towards supervision
- The supervisor receives complaints or requests for help from the employee's colleagues or family members

The more symptoms noted the more serious may be the difficulties, at least in some situations. But there are other sources of information the supervisor can tap in the interest of helping a troubled employee. Peers may know what's going on well before the supervisor does. Some gentle probing by the leader is in order when something seems amiss. You might be amazed at how much you learn if you simply ask.

The employee himself is, of course, the best source of information for the leader who wants to help him. Gentle questioning is the key here, too. It's up to the supervisor to approach the employee privately, note that "things just don't seem to be right," and ask some questions about what is going on. It may take some persistence on your part. You know police people and you know well how many of them resist and resent what they see as "meddling," no matter how well intentioned. You'll also have to be the best judge of when to back off and try again later. Do not be surprised if you encounter stiff resistance or even outright hostility before finding out anything at all. But the counselor-leader who wants to help will persist unless and until it is absolutely clear his concern is unfounded. You can't help if you can't know.

Just as cops are not social workers but nevertheless do a great deal of social work, you are likely not a trained employee counselor but will find yourself in the role of one, perhaps more often than you would prefer. Common sense can take you as far in this role as it does in so many of the other tasks you successfully master. Many times, all you will need to do is offer a readily available, patient, noncritical ear to a troubled soul who just wants to talk. More than a few troubles have been diminished through the simple act of being heard by a sympathetic listener who doesn't interrupt or offer seemingly-obvious but perhaps impractical solutions ("Just stop doing it.").

Granted, the problems that can be vanquished by talking and listening may be the easier ones. Others will require definite, concrete action by the employee before they can be solved. Here you can continue to listen and offer some of your own ideas that might help. It is important, however, that you do not take on the responsibility of solving the problem. It must remain clear to your subordinate that he is the one responsible for that. You still can offer advice as well as resources for the weightier issues. An employee with marital issues likely needs to avail himself of the services of Employee Assistance or a private marriage counselor. A cop with an alcohol problem needs professional assistance, such as Alcoholics Anonymous. All of these referrals you can make.

There are many more sources of professional help available today. Your Human Resources Department or United Way should be able to identify those available locally. Your job is not to drag your troubled employee there, but to make the location of help known to him. The rest is up to him.

Of course, counseling involves more than being a good listener, as vital as that skill may be. Often your job as counselor will require you to tell an employee something that he does not want to hear, and probably doesn't agree with. But that, too, is part of your job as a leader: correcting conduct not in keeping with the police organization's needs, standards or expectations. It won't always be easy, but here are a few guidelines to help make it as effective as possible for its intended recipient:

- Find a private place to do it; counseling is not a spectator sport.
- Be sure you reserve enough uninterrupted time to do it; employee counseling meetings can go a lot longer than anyone planned.
- During a counseling session, avoid emotional trigger words such as "lazy" and "dishonest."
- Be ready to try another approach if you encounter strong resistance.

- Keep your voice calm and at a normal, conversational volume level.
- Don't be shocked and overreact if you meet strong and emotional opposition, ranging from tears to a verbal attack against you.
- Avoid a massive show of authority ("I'm the boss!") whenever possible.
- Remember that most police people are Type AAA personalities who will react badly if they feel they are being "talked down to" or bullied.
- Keep reminding yourself to listen more than you talk.
- Don't let your own ego get caught up in your counseling efforts.
- Repeat yourself if your message clearly is not getting through, but don't keep doing it endlessly.
- Don't lessen or relax your reasonable demands just because your employee disagrees with them.
- Realize that a counseling session doesn't have to have a "winner" and your subordinate is not duty-bound to agree with you.
- Be prepared to call an intermission and resume the session, even on another day, if emotions and rhetoric are getting overheated.
- Agree on what you can; be agreeable to talking again later after your subordinate has the opportunity to think about what was said.
- Follow up to see if required change is actually occurring and continuing.
- Know that formal disciplinary measures may be required if the employee fails to respond favorably to your counseling directions.
- Realize that an employee's failure to respond to counseling is not *your* fault.

No, you are not a counselor. But expect to spend more than a little of your time in counseling duties. The preceding list of commonsense guidelines will help you succeed when you must hang out your counselor's shingle. As your experience has already taught you, counseling will always be part of what a leader does. Try to condition yourself to welcome the challenge as one more way in which you can tangibly help your people, your organization and the community you all serve.

YOUR ROLE AS A PLANNER

Every law enforcement leader engages in planning of one sort or another. The chief and his command staff team may work on putting together a strategic plan that is intended to guide the department for the next three to five years. The division commander may be making plans to shift mid-managers around to achieve his own goals. You, meanwhile, as a first-line leader will have planning of your own to do.

Every supervisor plans, even if he doesn't take the time to think that he's doing it. His planning is almost certainly both short- and long-term in nature. This morning he may be planning how to get all of his unit's patrol cars to the radio shop for needed maintenance. At noon he may be planning how he will guide his people in serving an arrest warrant on a fugitive known to be a flight risk. Towards the end of the shift he may be planning next month's personnel deployment on the street as vacation season gets into full swing.

The first-line leader is also participating in the exercise of planning when he finds an appropriate school for his subordinate who shows a need for strengthening in a certain area of the job. Here his responsibilities to plan and train become intertwined as he helps prepare an employee to better succeed well down the road, thereby strengthening both the individual and the organization. He is doing the same thing when he gives a supervisor-wannabe the chance to lead under his close oversight. He is helping train an individual as a leader-to-be, but he is simultaneously helping plan the department's future, however indirectly it may feel at the moment.

The smart supervisor will make it known to his own boss that he is willing and able to take on planning assignments that go beyond single team or unit needs. By taking on the additional work under your boss's supervision you will accomplish more than making him happy by taking a task off his shoulders. You also will learn and practice an additional skill while showing management that you are capable of handling new responsibilities. The product of your planning efforts does not have to be perfect (few plans are) so long as you learn from the experience, and make it plain that you did. The point is that you have now shown the brass that you are willing to take on additional responsibilities. That won't hurt when performance reviews, promotions and special assignments are under consideration.

Engaging in planning efforts for the benefit of your department is important. It is no less important to plan for your own future. The most successful leaders have a self-generated roadmap of where they intend to go. You should have one, too. It should include the career stops along the way and details on how you plan to get to each. That's where your planning for formal education and training is added to your overall plan. Some leaders commit their carefully-crafted plan for the future to paper; others keep it in their head. You should do whatever works best for you, but do *something.* Your plan, even with an unplanned, temporary diversion or two along the way, should become your future.

YOUR ROLE AS A "RIFLEMAN"

The United States Marine Corps has a number of great traditions. One goes like this: "Every Marine a rifleman first." The phrase simply means that when things get tough, whether you happen to be a cook, clerk, pilot or general, you are expected to be capable of picking up a rifle and joining the fight. American troops in World War II generally held in highest regard the leaders who carried a weapon and shared in front-line combat dangers, at least on occasion.

It is very likely that your own troops expect you to be able to be a "rifleman," too. That doesn't mean that they want you to be out there doing traffic stops and turning over perps to them on a regular basis. By doing that a lot you are only creating more work for them. However, they probably do want you to back them up and provide hands-on assistance when it is called for. They expect that you'll know what to do when you arrive on their scene. They want to know that you'll help with the menial or hazardous tasks, when necessary. And they don't want to have yet one more naive spectator to look out for because you have arrived on-scene.

Being a competent "rifleman" doesn't just pertain to expectations placed upon the patrol sergeant by his troopers. If you are a detective supervisor or lead police personnel in some other specialized assignment your employees will expect you to know enough about their jobs that you can lend a genuinely contributing hand when necessary. It is not reasonable for them to expect you to do their jobs *for* them; it is quite reasonable for them to expect you to help.

If you've been in a restaurant, auto parts store or some other establishment during peak business hours, you have probably noticed that good bosses join in the work, whether that means swabbing tables or lugging merchandise. In doing the "grunt" work when needed they earn the respect of their employees. You should do no less in a profession where the respect of your subordinates is vital. Doing so also contributes to your efforts to serve always as an excellent role model.

Never forget how to do the job. It's why you became a law enforcement officer in the first place.

SUMMARY

You can be forgiven if you see the list of duties of a first-line leader as practically endless. It probably feels that way, too. In addition to the expectations placed upon you to lead, train, and otherwise prepare your subordinates for the challenges of the job, you also can expect to be held responsible for the "other duties as assigned" part of your job description. You probably know already that the list of "other duties" is limited only by the imagination of your own supervisor.

You have yet other responsibilities to your people, too. You will be expected to correct and discipline them, when necessary. You will be expected to represent their interests to upper management. You probably will be held accountable for investigating the complaints against your people levied by unhappy customers. And, of course, there's more.

To do the best job of leadership possible while maintaining your own physical and emotional health, you will need to reach a reasonable balance in paying attention to your many tasks. You will need to be a wise time manager in determining how many minutes to accord each one. You will need to be able to recognize that not all tasks are of equal importance or gravity. You will have to be able to prioritize quickly and intelligently. Only by sorting your jobs out in this way can you get your vital work done while maintaining your own equilibrium. The job can only make you crazy if you let it!

Properly balancing your many important tasks will require your full attention and best planning efforts. If after thought you are unable to ascertain what appears most important in the scheme of things, do not hesitate simply to *ask* your boss what he or she sees as the priority of the moment. Your boss wants the task done right and done on time. It's hard to imagine that your supervisor would hesitate to provide you this reasonable guidance. Ask for it when you need it. You could save yourself a lot of wasted effort and unnecessary worry in the process.

Keeping your tasks balanced will aid you in keeping your life at and beyond work well-balanced, too. It's what you owe yourself in order to work and live in good health.

Chapter 4

HOW TO BE A GREAT ROLE MODEL
FOR YOUR TROOPS

You have doubtlessly noticed it: today's police employees are unlike those who have preceded them. That may feel at first blush like an understatement. They are not better or worse, but different. Most are willing to give you, their supervisor, their very best efforts. But they expect quite a lot in return.

One thing these police people of today expect is that you, their supervisor, will demonstrate the qualities that you demand of them. The old "do as I say do, not as I do" will not work for them. They expect more, and rightfully so. They expect you to model for them the personal characteristics and behavior you require them to copy. They expect you, in other words, to be a role model. You already know that you cannot afford to be anything but a positive one.

It is your task as a leader to demonstrate always what you expect of your subordinates. You know this, too: demonstration is one of the most effective modes of instruction. Setting a good example is what being a supervisor is all about. It works whether you are laboring on an auto assembly line, in a meat packing plant, or on the mean streets of America as a first-line police supervisor. You set the standards through your own demonstrated character traits, personal behavior and job-related skills and knowledge. You are the one that the young cops should look to in determining what kind of officer they aspire to be.

There is a lot resting on your shoulders as a positive role model. The task is not an easy one. Being a terrific role model all of the time does not permit you a lot of slack. You are almost always "on." It probably feels like you are allowed very little room for error. But you accepted that responsibility when you accepted the insignia of your rank. Serving as the best possible role model is not beyond your capabilities. It can be done and done well. Here's how.

WHAT IS A ROLE MODEL?

A role model sets an example of how he expects others to be. When the term is applied to law enforcement supervision, it refers to the conduct that a leader engages in that he wants his subordinates to emulate. It refers not only to how he does his job but how he lives his life, as well. Being a role model means that you are always on display, whether you are on-duty or off. It means that what you do with your personal time is just as important as what you do with your employer's time, at least in the eyes of your people. And, of course, it's a role model for *positive behavior* that you are seeking to be.

Every line of work needs a good supply of positive role models. In a business where the safety of the public and your employees is often at stake, the need for positive examples established by leadership is even more vital. Setting a poor example literally could get someone badly hurt — or worse. You don't want *that* weighing on your conscience forevermore.

You are looking to set a good example for everyone witnessing your actions, but most especially you are doing it for your subordinates, the people who should learn how to do the job right by following your lead. You know already that your people look to you for what they should do, how they should act. You never want to disappoint or mislead them by providing a poor example.

How do you serve as a positive role model? For one thing, you do things the right way without cheating or taking inappropriate shortcuts. You always give more than you have to. You avoid earning a reputation for doing "just enough." That may mean that you routinely get there early and, when necessary, stay late to get the job done. That holds true whether you are getting paid for every second of your time or not. You do things right, but you also do the right thing. Always.

There are a lot of other ways in which you serve as a positive example. You demonstrate the technical skills you want your people to have. That could include firearms skills or how you pilot a police vehicle in a safe manner. In that respect you serve as a smart risk manager, too.

By setting a good example for mature and responsible behavior you may prevent one of your charges from injuring himself – or someone else – through unsafe behavior.

Naturally, you always display excellent officer safety skills and demand that your people do the same. You promptly and effectively deal with unsafe behavior. If you realize that *you* have acted unsafely, you acknowledge the error to your officers and assure that they know the right way to do it. Meanwhile, you must display the comprehensive knowledge of the laws, policies and procedures that your troops must master to do their jobs well. It's alright for you to answer their questions, but ultimately you must direct them to learn the answers for themselves.

Additionally, you need to model great human relations skills – people skills – and require your people to copy them. Nothing is more vital to a peace officer than learning to treat others with empathy and respect as well as firmness and directness when called for. Your good example can help them learn which to use and when to use it.

Your employees should learn professional police ethics and build upon their personal moral base by observing you, on-duty and off. Once more, by your excellent example you can help them become what the profession needs more of: ethical, moral, competent peace officers. At the same time, by watching you your officers can learn the importance of loyalty to the organization and profession you all serve. From their observations of you these employees can have driven home to them that it is never alright to betray what you stand for and belong to by immoral or unethical behavior. Indeed, from you they can learn a lot that can help them survive the next 25 years on the job and emerge unscathed in body and soul.

By your attitude, performance and speech you are helping mold law enforcement's future. It may sound corny or trite, but it is absolutely true. By watching your example and listening to what you have to say your subordinate should be able to determine what kind of cop he or she aspires to be. That's reason enough right there for you to always seek to set a good example.

There's yet more you can do to serve as a positive role model for your troops. You never cheat or fudge on the rules. You don't accept favors or benefits that you deny to your people. You remember always that there's one set of rules for everyone. You are not "special" because you're the boss. You avoid doing things that you would punish your subordinates for doing. Double standards have no place in a professional law enforcement organization.

Even the best supervisor, the most exceptional leader, makes mistakes from time to time. When you realize that you have erred, admit it. If an apology is in order, give it without hesitation. Your people will appreciate it and think more highly of you. Most important, it's the right thing to do. It is what a good role model would do.

WHAT KIND DO YOU WANT TO BE?

Another way of asking the same question might be this: What sort of example will you set for your watchful followers? Likely (and hopefully) you want to be the very best. But how are you to go about it?

Think of the best leader you ever watched in action. It could be a former boss or even a current one. It might be someone else in your department or your profession. Then again, it might well be someone in an entirely different line of work living in another time. It could even be a historical figure you have always admired. Or you may have several role models in mind. There's nothing wrong with picking the best traits from different people in putting together the kind of model you want to be. The point is to learn from the examples of someone else in constructing the role model that you will become.

Of course, you cannot be anyone else. Being yourself will have to suffice. But being the good person that you are should be plenty. No one is perfect. Chances are the leaders you most admire had a few flaws, too. You can elbow your own imperfections to the side by emphasizing and strengthening the good things you want your people to see. It's likely that they won't expect you to be perfect. Being human should work just fine.

The kind of role model you want to be should be one who is always striving to get better, to do better. He should be one who seeks to continuously improve his job knowledge, skills and abilities. He should be one who attempts to refine his people skills and get better at training, mentoring and coaching his employees. He should be the one who always reaches higher to be a better leader and a better person.

None of this is beyond your ability as a leader. All of this you are capable of doing as a role model. And as that positive role model, you may want to give some thought right now to the traits you want to possess and exhibit to those around you.

WHICH TRAITS DO YOU WANT YOUR PEOPLE TO COPY?

An effective leader is a lot of things. As a positive role model you will want to display these traits in your own actions and in the way you live your own life. These are the things that you want your subordinates to copy. They are the things that you are willing for the whole world to see, because they comprise what you are.

Every leader has a slightly different list of the traits he hopes to demonstrate to others. You will have your own, too. But if a poll were taken from successful role models enumerating the traits they would want to display to the world, it's highly likely that the following, admirable traits would be among them:

Loyalty. To your organization and your profession, that is. You realize that you are a part of a cause or a calling and you pledge not to embarrass or bring disrepute to either. You can't expect loyalty from your people if you don't first show them what it looks and feels like.

Truthfulness. As a law enforcement officer your earned credibility – the ability to be believed when you say something – is one of your most treasured possessions. The same holds true with your subordinates. They must have good cause to know that anything and everything you tell them is, to the very best of your knowledge, the truth. There is no acceptable substitute for the truth.

Personal courage. Yes, you must possess the guts to go into a darkened building along with your people in search of an armed offender. That's one form of courage that your people will expect you to possess. But as a leader you also must have the courage to deliver unvarnished bad news and enforce an unpopular rule or decision. You also must have the courage to apply the disciplinary process even when you may not fully agree with the discipline. Courage means doing the right thing even when it's hard.

Technically competent. Your people count on your being a subject matter expert that they can go to when they don't know what to do or how to do it. You don't have to do their work for them; you do need to be able to help them figure out how it is done. Remaining current and competent in your field is mandatory for a leader.

Good decision making. Your troops need to have confidence that the calls you make are the right ones. They need to know that your good judgment and decision-making skills will help keep them out of physical or legal danger. In other words, they need to know that you know what should be done and how it is to be done right. They need to know that you will be neither careless nor capricious in your decision making.

Ethical and honest. Along with the need for an earned reputation for believability you must have an unquestioned reputation for absolute integrity, on and off the job. You would not want to work for a crook or an unethical jerk. Your people don't want to, either. As a police leader your integrity must remain above reproach at all times. That is an absolute requirement for a supervisor.

Politically astute. Without becoming a politician you must have a politician's sense for the repercussions to be expected from what you and your people do. You expect your officers to let you know when they have arrested the mayor's son so that you can let *your* boss know. You still do what's necessary as an ethical peace officer, but you avoid having your chain of command surprised by your doing it. Part of being politically astute is being aware of who's who on the local political scene without extending any of the politicos any special privileges.

Empathetic. This isn't exactly the same thing as *sympathy.* You don't have to feel bad because your employee is going to be suspended without pay for a couple of days for poor behavior. He may richly deserve the punishment. But at the same time you can understand *why* he did what he did and feel sad that he did it. You can even let him know that you still value him as a person and a peace officer from whom you expect much better in the future. You also can let him know that what is done is done and it's time to move on to better things without dwelling on what is past.

Intelligent. Law enforcement today requires smarts – a lot of them. Your people need to know that you have studied your job thoroughly and are continuing to broaden your knowledge. They want and need to be proud of their boss. One way you can help them do that is by making good, fact-based decisions that affect their jobs. Another is by speaking intelligently and avoiding sounding like a profane bumpkin. You don't have to show off your intelligence deliberately. Just doing your job competently should help do the trick nicely.

Good sense of humor. Too many cops, a few supervisors among them, take themselves way too seriously. Oftentimes this shows through as arrogance or insecurity to those around them. At times they are referred to as being "badge heavy," and it's not intended as a compliment. Displaying a genuine sense of humor – including the ability to laugh at yourself and your own foibles – will go a long way towards placing those around you at ease. A good role model knows how to laugh at the appropriate times without coming across as mean or inappropriate to others. Appropriate humor can take the edge off of a tense situation. Don't lose the ability to laugh.

Fair. Your people and your employer expect you to have a strong sense of justice. That sense should be readily displayed in your day-to-day handling of your employees in all kinds of situations, including discipline-related ones. Legitimate accusations of partiality and favoritism in the way he treats his subordinates can be devastating to the reputation and future effectiveness of a supervisor. It may stop his career advancement, perhaps permanently. Resolve now to remain impartial at all times in your dealings with everyone, subordinates included.

Emotionally and physically fit. You want your people to follow your good example in showing the public what a professional peace officer looks, sounds and acts like. You can help yourself accomplish that goal by taking care of your physical and mental fitness. To do that you will need to establish a reasonable exercise and dietary regimen for your body. You'll need to do the same for your mind. Really work at maintaining a good attitude about your job and life in general. Have some friends to talk to who aren't cops. If you sense that you ever need professional mental help, don't be ashamed to secure it. (You wouldn't be ashamed of a broken leg, would you?) Go get the help you need. Your people need *you.*

Forgiving. A good leader is willing to let past mistakes and grievances go. That doesn't necessarily mean he forgets them, but neither does he continue to stew over them and plot revenge. He knows that's not healthy. Whether he is traditionally religious or not, a smart supervisor realizes that maintaining and constantly rehashing old grudges and grievances is bad for him. It's not what a good role model does. It's not something that his impressionable people need to see. Let it go.

Exceptional communicator. The successful supervisor is highly skilled in both written and oral communication. He realizes the importance of understanding as well as the damage and inefficiency that can result from a misunderstood supervisory direction or other communication. You realize it, too. Strive to communicate clearly. Ask questions to assure that you have been understood. Repeat yourself, if necessary. Never stop trying to get better at delivering the written and spoken word clearly. Know that every great leader is also a great communicator.

This roster of highly admirable traits may appear to be describing the true Renaissance Man or Woman, not you. But it *can* describe you, or at least it should. Remember, there is no expectation or requirement that you must be perfect. Probably no one is. But by doing your best to serve as an exceptional role model for your law enforcement subordinates you can come acceptably close to reaching that standard. These are the traits of a positive role model. These are the characteristics of a leader.

IT APPLIES OFF-DUTY, TOO

As a representative of your agency and a responsible police supervisor you are never really out of sight. Whether you are boating on the nearby pond or having a libation or two at a local restaurant there's a pretty good chance someone will recognize you. That's probably happening even when you don't know it. If you have had too much to drink or are in the midst of a loud and very public domestic argument, someone probably noticed. If they did, they are probably going to tell others. The information (or misinformation) will travel widely and almost certainly will get back to your organization, sooner or later. That's not going to help you in your effort to serve as a positive role model for your people and your organization. What is the obvious solution to the problem? *Don't engage in the bad behavior in the first place.*

If you want to retain your moral authority to require that your subordinates do the right thing, you cannot afford ever to set a poor example yourself. Yes, that can feel like a burden. But it is a burden you voluntarily accepted when you became a supervisor. The obligation to do the right thing extends beyond duty hours.

Someone in the department, perhaps you, probably told the latest crop of rookies about the video test, the requirement to live your life as if you were eternally on camera and your loved ones were watching the show. The video test applies to you, too. You should assume that not only your subordinates are watching. People who don't like you may be watching, as well. They'd like nothing better than laying you low by reporting on your less-than-sterling behavior. Deny them the ammunition they need for the rumor mill by assuring that your off-duty conduct is as guilt-free as your duty-related efforts.

Of course, there are some common sense things you can do to avoid placing yourself in a situation where bad and embarrassing things can befall you. It starts with not putting yourself someplace where your native smarts and life experience tell you bad things can happen. That includes the bar where the Friday Night Fights are a regular occurrence. It includes the after-watch party where there's a good chance somebody is going to get wasted and pick a fight – maybe with you. And it includes any other social event where your good sense tells you poor judgment and mischief will come to the fore sooner or later. All of these are places that the career-savvy supervisor will avoid. You don't have to worry about setting a bad example if you're not there to do so in the first place.

Inasmuch as you are a supervisor, there's always a chance you may have to sit in disciplinary judgment concerning something that happened at one of these poor judgment events. That will be difficult for you to do if you were contributing to the poor judgment, or at least witnessing its results first-hand. You thus have good reason to stay away beyond your need to be an excellent role model. It is also a lot more comfortable if you don't have to explain your actions or your presence later when your own boss is looking for explanations.

As your life experience may have taught you, almost as many cops end up losing their livelihoods through off-duty stupidity as lose them for on-duty misbehavior. You don't want to be one of them. You are apt to find that your organization has less tolerance for misbehavior by its supervisors than it does for similar actions by its first-line employees. That's fair enough. As a positive role model for your people you shouldn't expect anything less.

You practice good street survival skills even when you are off the clock. You always should practice excellent career survival also, regardless of your duty status at the moment. At the same time, you will be serving as an exceptional role model for your observant and always-learning subordinates.

SUMMARY

You are a recognized, formal leader in your law enforcement organization. None of your duties is more important than serving as an exceptional role model for those within and without your agency. When you are expected always to set a good example you are hardly ever totally out of sight. That requires that you not relax your vigilance and appropriate behavior for even a minute.

You do not have to be perfect. No one is. At the same time, you must remain alert to those unguarded moments in which you are tempted to do something (or fail to do something) that would cause you, your organization and your profession embarrassment. Missteps that are allowed the average citizen often are denied to you if you are to retain the moral high ground expected of a police leader. Keeping that high ground, of course, permits you to expect the same of your subordinates. All of those high expectations range from your drinking habits to your driving behavior to the way you live your not-so-private life. At times it may feel like too much, but it's worth remembering that no one forced you to accept your leadership role. You accepted it because you knew you could do it, and do it well.

You also must do more than avoid bad behavior. You must establish the gold standard for the way you do your job, too. You must be engaged fully in your agency and your community. You must display professionalism and courtesy to those you encounter. You do your job well. You never lose the knowledge and understanding and abilities that make for a good cop.

You are and must always be what you want your people to be. Most of your people want to be proud of their boss. Many will seek to replicate your behavior. It is up to you to look, sound and act like the law enforcement officer you want your people to be. That's how you serve as a great role model for the people who will follow you.

Chapter 5

HOW TO SUCCEED (OR FAIL) AS A LEADER

You have been a part of the law enforcement profession for a while now. During your time in the business you have seen leaders come and go. Some of them you probably have labeled as successful. One or two you may even have resolved to pattern your own career after. Others you probably have seen as failures, to one extent or another. These are the ones you have neither admired not felt any particular desire to follow. These individuals you may have decided were failed leaders.

What is the difference between successful leaders and those who fall short? What do the winners possess that those less successful lack? What are the things that you will need to have in good supply to succeed as a leader in your own organization and your own community? What, precisely, are the characteristics of an effective leader? Those are all reasonable questions and are ones you should be asking now.

Just as your patrol officers or investigators need a complete set of tools to do their jobs well, so, too, do you require a well-stocked toolbox to do your own job of being an exceptionally effective leader. You certainly know that some tools work better than others. A tool appropriate for one task may be worse than useless for another. Those same rules apply to the tools needed for leadership. Your leadership toolbox needs to be full of what you need to do your difficult job, and do it well. Exactly what needs to be in that toolbox is the next topic for discussion.

WHAT'S IN YOUR TOOLBOX?

An effective leader requires a wide variety of tools and tactics to do his job well. They include the following:

Command presence. You've always heard that you need it in order to be an effective supervisor, but exactly what is it? Command presence often is referred to as the readily-apparent ability to be in control of oneself and the situation at hand, regardless of the circumstances. It calls for visible self-assuredness that does not stray into arrogance. It involves a manner of speaking and even a way of standing or walking. It doesn't call for a ramrod straight backbone or strutting. It does rule out slouching around with your hands in your pockets.

Command presence requires self-control that prohibits over-the-top emotional displays. It outlaws timidity, but also denies you the ability to display disabling fear or panic. What you will instead seek to demonstrate is a quiet, take-charge demeanor that says "The boss has arrived. I'm in control; it's going to be alright."

Vision. If your eyesight is 20/20 that's great, but what your people and your boss need to see in you is your ability to envision what's going to happen down the road as a consequence of what you and your employees are doing right now. Vision requires that you be able to foretell the future, at least to some degree. For instance, you need to be able to predict with a good degree of accuracy the effects on productivity of a new policy on traffic enforcement or the effect on the department's ethical reputation brought about by a proposed lowering of hiring standards. You need to have vision that allows you to predict where you and your organization are going before either of you actually arrives there.

A really good supervisor will be able to help his employees see and share in a vision, whether it's vision for the watch or one for the whole department. Perhaps the vision is for improved customer service or a marked reduction of street crime in a specific area. The talented supervisor will guide his people to share in the vision and help develop a strategy for achieving it.

As an effective leader you will know where you want to lead your subordinates and have at least some idea of how you plan to get there. Oftentimes that's called vision. It will need to have a place in your leadership toolbox.

Credibility. Simply put, do you have a reputation for telling the truth or not? Your bosses and your subordinates must believe without question that what you are telling them is the whole truth and nothing but. In that way it's tied to the absolute mandate for integrity in every supervisor. You must tell the truth even when it feels temporarily more comfortable to hold back. If you lie, very likely the pain will come later.

There will be times when telling the harsh truth will make those who hear it angry, sad or disappointed. But you gave up the dubious privilege of shading the facts when you became a supervisor. Being trusted as a truth-teller at all times is a must for a successful leader. Developing a reputation as a liar – even one who lies by omission or degrees – will destroy your ability to be an exceptional leader. Truth should always be your hallmark.

Reliability. A close relation of credibility, reliability means that when you say you are going to do something you actually do it. A good leader practically exudes reliability. Reliability also means that, beyond keeping your word, you get something done *when* you said you would get it done, not ten minutes or ten days later. An absent reputation for reliability can offset just about any positive traits you may have in your toolbox. If your boss cannot rely on what you said or promised you are of greatly decreased value to him or her. That's not the route you want to take in establishing an earned reputation as an effective leader.

Integrity. There is probably no more important characteristic for a law enforcement leader to display than a reputation for honesty and integrity. There is no more valuable tool in your box than this one. A law enforcement leader lacking integrity will not be a leader for long. While serving as a model of what your subordinates should aspire to be you always should present them an example of an individual who is moral, ethical and otherwise upright in all his dealings with others. The requirement applies to both your on- and off-duty life. It governs your personal dealings with the world as well as your professional ones.

Integrity means that you do the right things even when no one is watching. It means that you do the right things *especially* when no one is watching. You cannot do less when you expect your charges to do the right thing at all times. Integrity can be catching. It's what you want your employees to develop from their close association with an ethical leader. That's you.

Courage. Not the sort that enables you to chase a bad guy down a dark alley, although you'll need that kind, too. You also will need the kind of personal courage that enables you to make a decision that you know will be unpopular, either with your subordinates or your bosses.

Sometimes this is referred to as administrative courage. Regardless, you will be required to have sufficient backbone to make the difficult calls and accept responsibility for having made them rather than attempt to lay them off on someone else. The difficulty attached to decision making is also multiplied when the decision turns out to be the wrong one, whatever the reason. Once again it requires courage to accept the decision as your own, made in good faith with the best information you had available. Neither your people nor your own supervisor will expect you to be right every single time. They *will* expect you to have the courage to own your actions and decisions.

Common sense. It has been defined as informal knowledge based on intuition, training and life experience. It's the sort of sense that tells you that you'll burn your hand if you stick it too near the fire. It's the intelligence that warns you that you or your people will get in trouble or be endangered if you or they follow (or fail to follow) a certain course of action. Common sense can be the little voice telling you to do or not do something.

Some people have a lot more common sense than others. Those with an ample supply of it tend to be better leaders. You will need plenty of it in your toolbox if you are to be an exemplary leader. Apply what life has taught you to your daily decision making. Listen to the "little voice." There's an extremely good chance that you will be a more successful leader for having done so.

Job knowledge. Your people won't expect you to be the most skilled cop on the street or the brightest investigator in the detective bureau. They *will* expect you to have a good cop's street sense. They *will* expect you to know how to work a case. They *will* expect you to be able to join in and do the job when the situation demands, even if you are not normally considered a "working" supervisor. The truth is that none of that is too much of them to ask.

You cannot afford to come up short in your knowledge of the laws, tactics, techniques, policies and procedures that guide the operations of your agency and your profession. Your people need to know that you have done the job and can do it again, when necessary. They need to know that you understand the intricacies of the tasks for which you will be evaluating their performance. They need to know, in other words, that you still know how to be a cop. Not a super cop, but an effective one.

Tact. An experienced peace officer knows that one doesn't anger people and bruise feelings any more than necessary. Doing either can make his job a lot harder. The veteran supervisor knows that the same advice holds true for the employees he leads. For that reason, he praises in public and corrects in private where his people are concerned. The experienced leader also has learned that it is possible to get his message across without dropping any of the emotional-trigger words that are practically guaranteed to stir up anger and resentment in the employee recipient. (Examples of hot button terms include lazy, unethical, dumb and careless.)

A thoughtful, tactful boss chooses his words with care. By doing so you can make your own job easier by minimizing opposition and conflict at the same time you treat an employee in a humane fashion. A good boss also realizes that there are times to confront issues and other times when the wisest course of action is to wait until emotions have cooled. As that "good boss" you will know when and where to challenge employee behavior and how to do it. It's all part of being a truly humane as well as a highly effective leader.

Impartiality. You always have been just in your dealings with the denizens of the streets. As a successful leader you must be no less fair in your handling of your police employees. That requirement for absolute impartiality applies to the performance reviews you prepare, the discipline you assess and the recognition you hand out for work done well. It, in fact, applies to every single action you take with a subordinate throughout the workday. There is no ethical room for exceptions to the mandate for fairness.

Any action you take or decision you make as a supervisor misses the mark as "the right thing to do" if it is not also fair to all of those concerned. An appreciation for the need for impartiality in all things will have to be one of the most important items in your leadership toolbox.

Empathy. Nothing says you should support or defend a bone-headed decision or action perpetrated by one of your subordinates. At the same time, as a fellow human being you can understand *why* he did what he did. That empathy may figure in your decision concerning how to best respond to the miscue.

Empathy is not really the same thing as sympathy. But being imperfect yourself, you clearly can appreciate what may have led to a "bad" or foolish deed on someone else's part. Indeed, you may have even fallen victim to the same error yourself at some point in your life. That understanding may help you aid an employee in surviving the mishap with his self-esteem (and his job) intact. It's all a part of truly caring about the "others" who make up your organization and who just may happen to work for you.

Ability to communicate. You have heard this before, and it is absolutely true. You may have been among the supervisors who have lectured rookie cops about the need to communicate well if they want to succeed in their new career. The same holds true for the leader who also wishes to excel. You can be the smartest, more technically competent, most caring supervisor on the planet. If your troops and your bosses cannot comprehend what you are trying to communicate to them, you will not succeed as a leader.

Never stop working to improve your abilities at communicating both orally and in writing. If you need to join Toastmasters or take a speech class, do it. If you need to sign up for some courses in order to improve your writing skills, do that. Practice both skills every chance you get. You get better at talking to groups by doing it. You produce a better written product through repetition, too. If necessary, come up with a mentor who will coach you and critique your communication efforts to help you get better. But do whatever you need to do to perfect your personal communication skills. It will be worth the effort for the peace of mind it brings you as you observe your own improvement.

HOW TO FAIL THE TEST

As you know all too well, there are also weak and failed leaders out there. Some of them work in law enforcement, although oftentimes both their subordinates and their superiors wish that they didn't. You don't wish to join their ranks. Instead you want to avoid their mistakes. Steering clear of those pitfalls is easier if you know in advance what they are. They include the following:

Playing favorites. One of the quickest ways to lose the respect and support of your subordinates is to show favoritism in how you treat them. That does not mean that you must treat a long-time friend more harshly than the others, as that will earn you hostility, as well. Someone should not be punished because the two of you are friends. But you shouldn't have "pets," either. The simple fact is that every one of your subordinates must be treated the same when it comes to handing out assignments, rewards or discipline.

Your handling of your subordinates must be based on their actions and their job performance, not on the nature of their relationship with you. When it comes to discipline, that does not mean that everyone receives exactly the same penalty for the same misdeed. That employee's past performance and attitude towards the offense must be examined in devising your response. Someone who has committed three previous "fouls" should not be treated precisely the same as the employee who has tripped up for the very first time. But however you elect to handle the indiscretion must not be based in any way on your pre-existing relationship with the individual. That's what true impartiality demands.

Lack of self-control. You don't like being yelled at or belittled, especially in front of others. Chances are your people don't much like it, either. It's only human to occasionally get really angry. But getting mad at your charges and acting on it for all to see and hear will get you in deep trouble as a supervisor. Displays of anger are not a luxury you can afford as a leader. They will diminish you in the eyes of your subordinates.

As a leader you may encounter a situation where immediate correction is needed in order to ensure public or employee safety, or to prevent an act which would be illegal, unethical or both. Take that action, as required. But the action should not include an out-of-control dressing down of your employee in a public place. Good leaders don't do those things. Correct in private and, even then, stay in control of your tongue and your emotions. You will be a better leader for it.

Lying. You expect your subordinates to tell you the truth at all times. Indeed, law enforcement today requires that all peace officers tell the truth without exception. You should therefore not be surprised to learn that your people expect you to refrain from lying to them, no matter how good your motives for lying might be, at least in your own mind.

Stretching the truth may lead you to think that you have avoided an uncomfortable situation, at least for the moment. Chances are the comfort won't last. Lies have a way of getting found out most of the time. When that happens, things have just gotten a lot worse. You will not be seen as trustworthy or effective by either your subordinates or your boss once you have earned a reputation as a liar. Tell the truth. It's easier, even though it may not feel like it at the time. It is also the right thing to do.

Setting a bad example. You want to serve as a positive role model for your troops, not a negative one. As a police leader you cannot hold your people accountable for doing the right thing while you don't. Failing in such a manner is a cardinal sin for a law enforcement supervisor.

There are practically limitless means for serving as a poor example. Not telling the truth, taking forbidden procedural or legal shortcuts, disobeying the rules and even using inappropriate language are examples of bad examples that come quickly to mind. There are plenty more. Remain alert and strive to catch yourself before you fall prey to one of these damaging mistakes. Your people will benefit from your will power and you'll feel better about yourself.

Absence of loyalty. A supervisor who clearly displays that he cares a lot more about his own welfare than that of his employees will not long succeed as a leader. Your employees have a right to expect that you will look out for their interests. That doesn't mean that you cover up for them when they do wrong. It does mean that you do your best to assure that they are treated justly, have what they need to do their jobs and are looked after by their boss: you.

You would not want to see a family member mistreated by anyone. You would seek to aid him or her in time of need. Your subordinates are your work family. They merit your care and consideration, too. In showing your loyalty to them you will treat them firmly but fairly, and expect others to do the same. Only in that way will you deserve the loyalty that your people show you in return. Loyalty must extend both ways.

Holding a grudge. It's normal that you like some people better than others. It is equally natural that you will recall the instances in which you feel that you were treated badly by others. It is likewise not inhuman to want to "get back" at them for their transgressions. The fact is, however, that you cannot hold a grudge accompanied by a desire for revenge and then take out that ill will on one of your charges who has offended you. That's not what a good supervisor does. It is certainly not what a leader does.

It is not abnormal to hold a grudge. But acting on one is beneath what you should expect of yourself as a law enforcement leader. You are much better than that. Let it go. You'll be a better leader (and a better person) for it.

Cheating. Every rule that applies to the people you lead applies to you, too. Being the boss does not grant you special privileges, at least not in that regard. You are a positive role model. You must adhere to the legal, ethical and procedural obligations of your profession even more than your subordinates do. You are, after all, the one they should model themselves after.

As you likely have learned, it is not always easy to be positive role model 24 hours a day, on duty and off. But it's part of being an ethical leader. To be that leader, you cannot grant yourself things denied your subordinates. You cannot fudge even a little on the rules you expect them to follow. You can't cheat. Not ever.

BUILD UPON YOUR SUCCESS

A great deal of energy has been put into a continuing discussion as to whether true leaders are born or made. Those who favor the "born leader" philosophy suggest that some people through seemingly "built-in" traits or aptitude are destined to be leaders in whatever environment they find themselves. There is little doubt that intelligence and self-confidence strengthen a leader, but whether these things are "natural" or learned is another topic that could be debated at length.

What IS clear is that you can bolster your abilities as a leader by studying your job and remaining always open to learning new things about how to guide and direct others. Leadership classes and seminars and books like this one can help you with that chore. But as in everything else you do as a trained observer, do not hesitate to be critical about what is being presented to you as "the gospel" about leadership. As life experience has taught you, some advice is better than other advice. Examine what you see, read and hear critically. If, after careful study, it just doesn't feel right (or helpful) to you, there is a good chance that it will not benefit you. Take everything in, but then sort through the material for what will be most helpful to you. You are not a clone of anyone else and what helps some other person may not be as useful to you.

You also can learn a lot by talking with and observing the actions of acknowledged leaders. Some will display character traits and abilities that you will want to copy. Others will say or do things that you will resolve never to do yourself, as they are unhelpful or simply wrong. (Regular display of an out-of-control temper would provide a good example.) You can learn from poor leaders and bad examples, too. One successful police chief reported that he learned what kind of chief he wanted to be by cataloging the mistakes of other law enforcement leaders he had observed over a career – and resolving never to commit them himself. He also filed away for future use the successful practices of a lot of police leaders. Not surprisingly, he confessed to oftentimes finding both positive and negative examples in the same person. You can do the same.

SUMMARY

Great leaders display vision, loyalty to organization and subordinates and plentiful supplies of common sense. They tell the truth and display personal courage in the face of adversity or threat. They know the job at hand and are willing, when required, to help their people get it done. They demonstrate honesty and integrity in all things, but most especially in their relations with their subordinates and supervisors. They admit their errors and endeavor to fix them properly.

Leaders are patient and show tact and diplomacy in their dealings with others. They are slow to anger. They are fair and impartial. They steadfastly display command presence and self-confidence without crossing the line into arrogance. They consciously groom their people to be leaders one day. Meanwhile, they strive to learn their own boss's job so they can help him today and perhaps take on his role later.

You are or are capable of being and doing all of these things. At the same time, you are studiously avoiding committing the all-too-common mistakes of a weak or failed leader. You avoid playing favorites, holding grudges and punishing those you don't like. You never engage in fits of temper or extreme frustration in front of your charges. You steer away from gossip and rumor-mongering and expect the same of your people. You never cheat or bend the rules. You do the job right and likewise bar your employees from engaging in improper shortcuts that you would never utilize yourself.

It's no secret that the subordinates of a strong and effective leader display higher morale than those of a weak or incompetent one. You know that by leading your people effectively you benefit them, the larger organization and the profession of which you are all a part. That is precisely how you succeed as a leader in your ever-challenging field.

Chapter 6

HOW TO COMMUNICATE EFFECTIVELY

As a human being it is very hard for you *not* to communicate. You do it even when you speak nary a word. You communicate when you smile at your significant other or scowl at your misbehaving five-year-old. You communicate when you cease reading the briefing notes in roll call until the jokers in the back of the room settle down. And you confuse more than you communicate when you tell Officer Jones that it is OK that he takes off Friday night at the same time you shoot him a look that says it's not really alright, after all. Indeed, you must be just about unconscious in order not to communicate.

Communication may be said to involve the transmission and, hopefully, the reception and comprehension of thoughts, feelings, ideas and information. Clear and effective communication is vital to the good health of any organization, yours included. Good communication between you and your subordinates figures in more than just the efficiency and effectiveness of your law enforcement agency. It also contributes to something else that every organization needs: high morale among employees. People who feel left out of what's going on tend to display low morale. Employees who are informed, included and "in the know" are more likely to feel a part of the organization and its mission. Often, they self-report being more satisfied with their job.

A good supervisor recognizes the value of the clearly written and spoken word. He realizes that effective communication makes for a more cohesive and productive work unit. He sees the worth of communication. *You* are a good supervisor. You see it, too. As a result, you seek to communicate to the very best of your ability at all times. You likewise work hard at assuring good information flow among your peers, bosses and subordinates. This chapter will help you contribute to that hoped-for organizational state of affairs where good communication rules.

HOW TO SUCCEED AT BEING MISUNDERSTOOD

Sometimes the best way to figure out how to do something well is to learn how *not* to do it. That approach will help you in becoming a more effective communicator. Experience teaches that there are a number of readily identifiable enemies of clear communication. They include these time-worn villains:

Bias and prejudice. If you feel you already know what someone is going to say because of your past dealings with him or her, you are unlikely to listen really carefully. If you dislike or mistrust someone for whatever reason, including a valid one, you are not likely to hear what he has to say this time without putting your own slant on his message. If you know in advance that you are going to disagree with whatever the communicator has to say because you have always disagreed with him in the past, it is unlikely that much effective communication is going to take place.

To overcome this communication bugaboo, it is up to you to try as hard as you can to set aside the past and focus only on what is being communicated right now. Only in that way will a message have a good chance of getting through intact.

Distractions. It can be physical or mental, but if you are distracted by something you are unlikely to receive clearly the communication that is being sent your way. The physical ones are the easiest to detect. A tangible distraction may consist of a yapping portable radio, a side conversation, a really noisy air conditioner, or another nearby disturbance of some kind. The intangible distractions may be harder to identify, but they exist all the same. A distraction can be found in your personal dislike for the communicator or your own focus on what you want to communicate in response. Whatever the case, distractions can keep the message from being received by its intended recipient.

It may be impossible to remove or neutralize every possible distraction. The world isn't a perfect place and neither are the people who inhabit it. But to the extent feasible it will be to your advantage to give your full attention to the primary business at hand while ignoring the sideshow.

Emotional involvement. Strong emotions can kill or deflect accurate communication. The emotion can be a positive one (great joy) or negative in nature (great sadness), it really does not matter. Whenever very strong feelings hold sway accurate information flow can get sidetracked. That doesn't mean that anyone is being intentionally uncooperative; it's simply how the human animal functions.

You cannot ban strong emotions from your world, even if doing so was a good idea. Instead, realize that when "big feelings" are asserting themselves you may find it necessary to repeat and clarify your message, such as a set of supervisory directions given at an officer-involved shooting scene. Check for understanding by asking questions ("Did you understand what we need to do?"). Be prepared to repeat or clarify more than once.

Inappropriate language. A poor choice of words can block effective communication as completely as blinders and ear plugs. Choosing inappropriate language for your audience can result in immediate opposition to what you have to say, whether you are speaking or writing. It also can give you a bad reputation and get you in trouble with your boss. Profane or vulgar language is something that you should ban from your speech. But not all inappropriate language consists of bad words. You also must avoid using terminology unlikely to be understood by your audience. You should not insult your roll call briefing by talking down to the troops as if they were young children. Neither should you write to them in terms best understood by a PhD. You are seeking to communicate, not impress people with your vocabulary.

Suit your words, spoken or written, to your audience of the moment. Again, check for understanding. Be prepared to adjust your approach if it appears that your readers or listeners don't get it.

Poor attitude. If you or your intended message recipient is simply not interested in what is being communicated, the message is unlikely to have the desired effect. This may tie back to preconceived notions or bias and baggage from the past. Whatever the cause, a poor attitude on anyone's part is a real communication killer. A bad attitude almost guarantees that the whole communication effort will have to be repeated. Even then it may not succeed if the negative feelings remain in place.

Even though you are a highly-responsible leader, there is no rule that says you must maintain a Mary Poppins attitude at all times and places. You are allowed to be human. At the same time, it will be worth your effort to try and set aside negative feelings and opinions long enough for a needed communication to take place. That's what adults have to do sometimes. Tough as it may be, give it a try for the communication benefits that will result. That, too, is what leaders do.

THE KEYS TO EFFECTIVE COMMUNICATION

Just as there are time-proven means of failing at communicating effectively, there also are experience-backed means for getting it right. There are a number of elements that must come together for a clear and effective exchange of thoughts, ideas and feelings to take place. They include the following:

Openness and credibility. You cannot communicate effectively if you simultaneously hide the truth, play word games and engage in other deceptive practices. Someone who is not believed cannot be a good communicator. Liars may be listened to but they are not heard. Say nothing as opposed to straining credibility. A reputation for a lack of credibility once established is hard to live down. Remain open and tell the truth, even when the truth feels painful to tell. Once the lies get out, as they generally do, your pain will be greater. You took an oath that calls for personal integrity. Remaining loyal to the truth is one way that you establish an earned reputation for integrity. Staying open and honest will help you be a better communicator regardless of your audience.

Two-way information exchange. For communication to succeed, all parties to the exchange have to know that their thoughts, feelings, ideas and information will be openly received by the others. That means everyone involved needs to have the ability to respond to and ask clarifying questions about the initial message. This back and forth must be allowed to continue until everyone has a chance to be heard. Diatribes that do not allow a response from the audience are generally not well-received and may be misunderstood, as well.

Effective communication allows information to flow both ways between sender and receiver. That reduces the likelihood of misunderstandings. It also is easier on the patience and attitude of each party to the communication. That makes for better communication, too.

Good communication habits. A lot of things could be included in any listing of positive communication traits or practices. Telling the truth leads the pack. Listening or reading patiently with filters turned off follows close behind. Keeping emotion-provoking words out of the message can help, too. Ditto for keeping the message clear, as short as possible and phrased in wording appropriate for the audience at hand.

Good communication habits are formed through practice, experience, and a genuine intent to play fair with others. Communication gets better with practice and without prejudice. It gets better by taking your time, picking your words carefully, and trying to keep your less-desirable emotions (like anger, for instance) out of your communique to the extent possible. Once you've broken your bad habits (poor listening skills, bias, shading the truth) you can spend even more time nurturing your positive ones. That, too, will make you a more effective communicator.

Clear message. Don't plug in a fifty-cent word where a dime's worth of clarity will work better. Keep it clear, keep it concise, keep it as brief as reasonable. Unfamiliar words are to be avoided or explained in the message. Long, involved sentences are to be avoided like Ebola. Oral presentations that drag on and on in a tortuous monotone are slow death and should be recognized as such. Remember the KISS principle: keep it simple, stupid. It actually works.

Don't try to force too many unrelated instructions or ideas into a single communication. Your audience may lose your message in the resultant sea of words. Tackle different topics one at a time, first checking to see if the last one was understood before you take off in a new direction. Remember that the average person's attention span is not unlimited.

Unemotional approach. Keeping your message factual will increase the likelihood of its being understood. That's not to say you cannot let your feelings show on occasion. Doing so shows your people that you are human. But getting carried away with excited rhetoric is likely to slow down understanding and distract your message's audience. Remain visibly calm and at least most of your audience is likely to take your cue and do the same. Honest emotions certainly have their place, but that place is probably not in the middle of an important communication from a leader (you!) to his subordinates.

No one wants you to act like a heartless machine. But staying in control of your feelings to a reasonable degree oftentimes will remove a major distraction as you seek to communicate effectively with those under your command. That all by itself will help assure that your earnest communication efforts are effective ones.

A leader who cannot communicate effectively commands and controls very little besides the desk or steering wheel in front of him. By being understood you greatly increase the likelihood that your leadership will be felt by your charges and result in the accomplishment of the goals and objectives you set for them. No leader can ask more than that.

SAYING IT IN WRITING

A really good leader is also a good writer. He has to be able to get his point across in many of the situations he will find himself in as a supervisor. In that role he will author memos, plans, orders, and performance reviews. Many things that require permanence call for a written record. A good writer provides that permanent record.

The written comments of the first-line supervisor can provide the evidence needed for the recognition or correction of an employee. Written documentation of specific acts and events provides the backing required for a personnel action of any sort. It also can command the attention of the supervisor's own boss when the writer is seeking to inform the brass of the need for change or some other action. A well-written communication can help inform and move others to accomplish needed change.

Not unlike many other things in life, one gets better at writing by writing, and doing lots of it. In order to get better at it you should critique your own work. Oftentimes it helps to place something you have written aside for a day or so. Then read it again and see if it looks as good or makes as much sense as it did when it was hot off the printer. Make changes where it makes sense to do so. Then, read it yet again with an eye towards further revisions. Read it one or more times for clarity of meaning. Then, read it again, slowly and meticulously, in search of errors in grammar, spelling, and factual content. Be comfortable that you have gotten it right before you send it forward.

Enlist additional eyes to critique your written work. A peer whom you know writes well can do it for you. So can your boss, once you tell him what you're up to: seeking to improve the written work product you submit to him. Rare is the boss who is not willing to help his subordinate improve his work. Doing that makes his own life easier, so he almost certainly will be willing to help you.

If you recognize writing as a weakness for you, avail yourself of courses that are available to help the "writing challenged" individual to write more effectively. Many very intelligent people need help with their writing skills, so do not feel badly about enrolling in a college writing class or on-line coursework. Your goal is to get better at what you will do a lot of as a supervisor, so don't be hesitant to invest a few bucks and a handful of hours and efforts. It should more than pay off in the long run.

As noted, you will get better at writing by writing. But don't just write. Be your own harshest critic. Carefully read what you have written down. Dissect your written work to eliminate unnecessary words. Double-check your spelling and grammar. Try to place yourself in the shoes of someone who doesn't have your knowledge of the subject and has no idea of what you are trying to communicate. Write and rewrite for that individual's level of understanding. In going through that exercise you will get better at placing your thoughts into written format.

SPEAKING TO BE HEARD

Face-to-face, oral communication skills are also a prerequisite for effective leadership. You must speak clearly and get your message across effectively if you are to realize your full potential as a leader. And just as in writing, you become more proficient at public speaking by speaking a lot in public, whether your audience amounts to two or two hundred.

The best public speakers call on words that are appropriate to the audience they are addressing. Words that may be well-received and understood by a roomful of college professors may not be equally effective for a gathering of patrol officers. That does not mean that one group is smarter than the other. It simply indicates that words and a manner of speaking appropriate for one audience may not work equally well for the other. It certainly does not call for the speaker to "talk down" to one group, or rely on profane or otherwise inappropriate language in an effort to make a point.

Oral communication has an advantage over the written word because speaker and listener alike will pick up cues on the feelings of the other. Facial expressions and other body language can help with the exchange. The in-person interaction also makes it much easier for the message-sender to grasp whether or not his message is being understood. In this environment, the communicator also can determine almost instantly the effect the message is having on its recipient(s). The intended audience can ask questions and seek clarification, if need be. The overall result of all of this should be improved communication and the benefits it brings to all concerned.

Speakers get better by speaking, whether in front of a patrol roll call briefing, or a gathering of the local Optimists. As in the case of writing skills, you can polish your oral communication abilities through adult education classes and college courses. Such coursework oftentimes comes with a critique of your speaking skills. With that kind of constructive criticism you can get better at what you do.

By being an effective oral communicator you can contribute to an atmosphere in which good communication can mean fewer misunderstandings, disagreements, and bad feelings among the employees of your police agency. This positive state of affairs is what you are seeking as a leader in the organization. You can help your department get there by both writing and speaking effectively.

Words, spoken or otherwise, can hurt and confuse as easily as they can inform and clarify. They can depress employee morale as well as elevate it. Communication, for better or worse, can help determine which way all of these things go. By functioning as an accomplished communicator you will make your law enforcement organization a more pleasant and positive place to work as well as a more efficient and effective one.

SUMMARY

As a competent leader you rely on good communication to boost the effectiveness of your work group and contribute to the overall efficiency of your organization. You know that a police agency where information and ideas flow easily and accurately is a better, stronger organization. You know that an organization of that kind probably will be staffed by informed, reasonably content employees. And you know, too, that in being a good communicator you contribute to the health of that organization and its individual members.

Good communication requires the full attention of both the message sender and his recipient. It requires good listening and reading habits and an attitude as free as possible of bias and preconceived notions. Finally, good communication requires the absence of distractions, prejudices, inappropriate language and excessively emotional statements.

As a leader, you must be an effective writer and speaker. It will be extremely difficult for you to succeed in leadership without both of those skills. You must be a good reader and listener, too. You must get the point of a message and you must be able to deliver your own points clearly.

Everyone in your organization as well as the public you all serve will benefit from good communication. Your people certainly will. There is little doubt that you will, too. When everyone understands everyone else things just naturally go more smoothly. And that happy condition is what every good leader is seeking.

Chapter 7

HOW TO EVALUATE EMPLOYEE PERFORMANCE: THE GOOD, THE BAD, AND THE VERY UGLY

The average supervisor would tell you that completing employee performance reviews or appraisals is not his or her favorite thing to do. In fact, many supervisors don't like to do them at all and wish that somehow the responsibility for doing them could be made to go away.

You are not the average supervisor. You realize that evaluating the work performance of your subordinates is a necessary and important task of a responsible supervisor. You realize that preparation of the performance evaluation document and the following meeting with its recipient are both important jobs and must be given the appropriate amount of time and effort to get it right. You recognize that it is the leader's job to complete reviews that are clear, unbiased, and informative. You know that the performance appraisal is vital to the health and the future of both the employee and the organization.

None of this is to say that your job as a performance evaluator is an easy one. Just about everyone – you included – is at least a bit apprehensive when he knows his work style, ethic and product are being evaluated. It is all too easy to come to the conclusion that it is *you* under scrutiny, not your work. And that thought brings all kinds of emotions into play. Being placed under the microscope in such a way is often not easy for either the evaluator or the very human subject of the evaluation. Nevertheless, it is an important job that must be done well. Most organizations go through the exercise once a year; some do it more often. Whatever the scrutiny schedule in your own agency, you must be prepared to do the job competently and fairly. This chapter will arm you with some common sense guidelines for doing just that.

WHY DO IT AT ALL?

If the person doing the evaluating and the one receiving the news both have expressed discomfort with the entire process, then why do it at all? Actually, there are some very good reasons for carrying out the performance review process. As a leader in your agency, you should be aware of them. The process, as you should know, is important and beneficial to employee and organization alike. For that reason, you must treat the whole process with the importance it is due.

All employees deserve to know how they are doing at work. You very likely feel the same way. Most people want to know what others think of what they are doing, although some will never admit it. The performance appraisal lets your employee know what someone important to him – you, his supervisor – thinks of his work. Whether he totally agrees with you or not, unless he's a very unusual character indeed he wants to know. Unless you are leading a very unusual work group, the majority of your employees will want to please you.

The performance appraisal lets an employee know where he can do better. If your agency connects employee performance to pay, as it should, your employee is able to learn from his evaluation session what he needs to do in order to obtain a reward, such as a step increase or bonus pay. If you have done the performance appraisal well, your employee also can learn from it what he needs to accomplish in order to attain promotion or a special assignment, if either or both of those things happen to be on his wish list.

Employees need to have goals and objectives on the job; many want them. Once more, you provide a good example of this very human desire. You almost certainly want to learn from your boss what you need to do to earn positive recognition, whether that recognition amounts to a monetary award, promotion, or a simple "attaboy." Most of your people want the same from you, whether they admit it or not. The reality remains that most people want to know how they are doing.

There's another reason for doing a competent, comprehensive performance appraisal for each of your subordinates. At some point in the future you may wish to reward or discipline them for past behavior. To do that you will require evidence, and that translates to mean documentation. The performance review or appraisal document is the place for that evidence. You have heard the expression "if it isn't in writing, it isn't." By putting evidence of past performance, good or bad, into written format you have made it part of the employee's history. That record can be used to offer solid backing for whatever personnel action you must take in the future. It's a good way to assure that whatever you elect to do tomorrow in the way of employee reward or sanction is very unlikely to be challenged successfully.

Well-done performance reviews also help the police organization in that they identify employees who are doing well, and may be good candidates for advancement and/or added responsibility. Competently-done reviews also identify employees who need additional coaching or other work if they are to remain a contributing part of the organization. By identifying both excelling and substandard performers, you as the supervisor involved also benefit your community of customers in that you are helping create a more efficient and effective law enforcement agency.

Performance reviews come in many formats, from the column of check-off boxes to the numerical scoring sheet to the nearly blank piece of paper that asks you to create a free narrative describing your employee's work-related behavior. Many reviews include a combination of all of these formats and add yet others. The format doesn't matter as much as the content. All can work well in the hands of a skilled evaluator. The key is that the comprehensive, honest review of past work gets done by a supervisor who realizes the great importance of the process and cares enough to do it well.

WHAT ARE YOU MEASURING?

Every law enforcement organization is different in some way or ways from every other, even though the similarities in what its employees do may be evident. As a result, a given agency may examine and evaluate employee tasks and traits that the agency just down the road does not consider to be as important. A good performance review will, of course, recognize these differences and ensure that they are given ample consideration in the performance review document and meeting. What's most important is what *your* organization sees as important.

At the same time, there are many areas of employee performance that will be the same from one place to the next, one organization to another. These are the areas that a complete performance review (and a good performance reviewer) should cover. As you go about preparing a comprehensive performance appraisal on one of your law enforcement subordinates, you likely will find the need to comment on most if not all of the following, in one way or another:

Technical job knowledge. How well does the employee grasp the technical aspects of his job, such as how to collect physical evidence or operate the devices connected with police work, ranging from the radio to the in-car computer? Can he safely and effectively use the weapons involved in law enforcement, including less-lethal options? Does he grasp the statutes, ordinances and court decisions pertinent to his position?

Agency policies and procedures. It's not enough to know the ropes; the successful police employee must also know the rules. Beyond that, how well does he follow the guidelines established to help him do his job safely, legally, and correctly? Significant rule or order violations occurring during the current performance appraisal period should be detailed in this section of the performance review. Your failure to record it means, in essence, that it didn't happen.

Job-related safety practices. Officer safety and survival is everything in the business of law enforcement. How well does the employee grasp the rules for survival on the street? What examples can you cite that provide evidence of good (or not so good) safety and risk management habits, preferably as seen through real-life incidents involving the employee? Does he show indications of learning from past lapses? What is he doing to prevent future mistakes? Is further training or corrective action indicated?

Customer service. Does the employee realize that law enforcement really does have citizen-customers? Does he appear to grasp the "Golden Rule" of customer service: treat others as you would want to be treated? Can examples be provided of past good or poor customer service delivered by the employee? Can he do something specific to do better in the future?

Communication skills. How complete and otherwise well-done are the employee's reports and other written work? How effectively does he communicate on the radio or telephone? Is he easily understood? Does the police employee appear to understand that his communication skills are among the most important talents he possesses to gain understanding and compliance from the citizens he encounters daily? Is he receptive to your efforts to help him boost his communication skills?

Knowledge of the area. In other words, can he find his way around the jurisdiction without too much trouble or delay? Can he generally get where he's going without help? Is he aware of the jurisdiction's problem spots and other places of "special interest?" If he has difficulties finding his way around, what is he doing to address the problem?

Judgment and decision making. Nothing is more important to a peace officer than sound, solid judgment in the face of calamity and mayhem. How does your employee do at decision making under stress? Can he generally make good decisions without calling a supervisor for advice? Just as important, does he know when to pause and seek advice? Does he have a reputation for good judgment and sound decision making? Once more, if you can cite concrete examples your performance appraisal will be much more helpful to its readers, including the employee himself.

Interpersonal relations. How well does the employee get along with his peers, supervisors and those he meets in the course of his duties? Is he moody and hard to get along with? Is he an impatient "hot reactor" apt to lose his temper with little provocation? Simply put, is he seen as a jerk or a nice guy? As always, examples will strengthen the evaluation document.

Professional appearance. This category looks at everything from personal grooming and cleanliness to the appearance of the employee's uniform or other clothing, depending on his or her assignment. Does the individual present the sort of public image that tends to bring positive comment from citizen onlookers – or not? The employee should strive to match the positive role model of professional appearance that you have set for him.

Acceptance of direction. Can the employee accept supervision, or is he likely to frequently challenge and question his supervisors? It is expected that an employee will ask clarifying questions and challenge illegal or unethical orders. But when questioning directions becomes routine for an individual, a problem is most often at hand. You need to cite specific examples if you have an employee who is doing poorly here. If this problem cannot be corrected, the individual is not fated for a long or happy future in policing. You will be doing him (and yourself) a favor by honestly confronting the issue now.

Teamwork. Law enforcement requires that its practitioners have the self-assurance to work solo when required, but the same people need to be able to contribute as part of a strong and cooperative team as necessary. A good team player is not a disruptive force on the team, nor does he allow others to do his share of the work. He participates in the group without attempting to dominate others. You will need to observe your subordinates working under various conditions and demands in order to make an accurate call in this area.

Attendance/punctuality. Is the employee where he is supposed to be when he is supposed to be there? If not, you must be able to cite the dates and times when he failed to meet expectations, assuming there is not a good reason for his absence or tardiness. You will earn the ill will of your other employees if you fail to deal with this shirker.

Self-confidence. As you know, in order to be effective at his difficult job a law enforcement officer must display self-assurance that does not cross the line into arrogance. It will be up to you to record whether or not each of your employees meets this key requirement. It will be helpful if you can cite specific instances in which a subordinate did or did not display self-confidence in his actions and decisions. Rating this particular factor should be done with great care and consideration. Tell the truth, but be prepared to back that truth with hard evidence.

DOING IT THE RIGHT WAY

You complete an appraisal of an employee's work performance in the same way you carry out your other responsibilities as a leader: with care, fairness, attention to detail and excellent communication skills. In that way the performance evaluation document and sit-down session both will provide maximum benefit to the employee and the organization as a whole. You can increase your chances of accomplishing that vital goal by adhering to some basic rules of thumb:

Set aside the time to do it right. It will not do justice to anyone if you rush your way through composing the performance appraisal document or hustle to get the sit-down session with its recipient out of the way. It may even help you to write the appraisal at one sitting, then set it aside for a day or two and read it again. The passage of time may tell you that certain points need clarified or otherwise revised.

Adequate, uninterrupted time and a quiet space also will be needed for the performance review meeting. The task must be seen as the important thing it is and should never be rushed, sidetracked or regarded as a distasteful chore. You should extend your employee the same time and consideration you expect from your own boss.

Consider using an outline. Some leaders find it helpful to do an old-fashioned topic outline to help them through the narrative portion of a written performance review. They say that doing so helps them organize their thoughts in an orderly, logical manner. Particularly if writing feels like a chore to you, you should try out the outline routine on a performance review or two and see if it makes the task easier. You may suddenly find evaluation-writing less of a bother.

Don't spring any surprises. It goes *almost* without saying: the performance review session should not be the very first time an employee has heard or seen a specific criticism from you. Emotional reactions often greet such an unwelcome surprise. For some employees the performance review session is already an uncomfortable affair. You don't want to add unnecessarily to the stress. You can avoid surprises by gently critiquing your employee's work and giving him or her progress reports throughout the year. These "warnings" have a very practical value in that they give him a chance to correct the problem or weakness.

Have the evidence and examples to back your statements. Every peace officer knows that you need evidence to prove a point. The same holds true during the performance appraisal process. It is acceptable to say that an employee has an attendance or punctuality problem. But the statement needs to be followed with dates and times when the problem surfaced. You can say that Patrolman Jones makes great felony arrests. In that case, examples of those arrests must be cited. Proving something by evidence and example is every bit as important in the evaluation session as it is in the courtroom.

Watch out for some common evaluation time errors. No matter what their vocation or profession, supervisors tend to make some of the same errors when it comes time to evaluate an employee's performance. Sometimes they let their personal prejudices and biases towards the employee get in the way. Or they fall victim to the so-called "halo effect" and cite only good or bad performance examples because one or the other is prominent. (Employees seldom do *everything* great or *everything* poorly.) Or they fall into the "central tendency" trap and mark virtually everything as "average" because it feels easier and seems to require less justification. Or they remember and comment only on what has happened recently and is fresh in mind, in spite of the fact that a major performance plus or minus occurred six months ago. Now that you know about some of the most common errors you can be sure not to make them.

Don't apologize for being honest. You shouldn't have to apologize for arresting someone who needs arrested. Neither should you have to say you're sorry because you did your job. Reporting accurately on employee performance is one of your most important roles as a leader. Employees cannot be recognized for exceptional work or held accountable (and fixed) for substandard performance without an honest and open appraisal from you, the supervisor who should know what they did and didn't do. Never apologize for your integrity.

Keep sentences and paragraphs short. The very best written performance appraisals are the ones that are easily understood by anyone who reads them. Don't use fifty-cent words where nickel ones will do. Avoid long, winding and complex sentences that go on for several lines. Your goal is to be comprehended by the individual you are writing about. Keep the document concise, clear and direct. Flowery language and philosophical speeches can be omitted, too. You are writing to communicate, not to impress.

Proofread your work. It would not be uncommon for you to comment on the accuracy and correctness of your employee's written work product. It thus would not do for you to commit your own spelling and grammatical errors in the appraisal document. Check your work for content. Then read it – carefully – at least once more, for mistakes in grammar or spelling. Be sure your facts are right, too. If in spite of all your caution you do make a mistake, let the employee know you are correcting it right away. Then, do it.

End with a summary that notes both strengths and weaknesses. Most readers like to have a summing-up provided at the end of a written document. Consider addressing a single, final paragraph to a message that sums up the employee's performance during the rating period as succinctly and clearly as possible. Try to include both the good and bad, assuming there is some of each. If possible, try to end on a positive note. (That likely won't be possible in the case of a truly failing employee.) It also may be helpful to close with a line that looks to the future, such as "Becky appears poised for a great year next year."

WHEN THINGS DON'T GO WELL

Try to set emotions aside. The very fact that their work product is being evaluated can be stress enough for some people. A few may arrive at the performance appraisal setting already girded for verbal combat. If you are in the same heightened state of alert yourself it's almost certain that things will not go well. It makes more sense to take a few deep breaths in advance, consciously calm yourself, and greet your employee with a pleasant demeanor that says you are not seeking confrontation. You might want to break the ice by talking about something else before getting into the performance appraisal and try to put the person at ease. Speaking in a calm, quiet voice you can then edge into the session itself. Continue to monitor your employee for any indication he or she may be getting agitated and be prepared to slow things down or even temporarily shift topics, if need be. Don't hesitate to enumerate the things your employee is doing well in addition to the areas where improvement is needed.

Be prepared for outbursts and venting. A visibly agitated employee who clearly doesn't feel he'll get fair treatment from either his employer or his supervisor may need to be given the opportunity to get what he has to say off of his chest. Your best bet may be to listen quietly without interrupting beyond an occasional nod of your head to indicate that you hear what he's saying and grant him permission to continue. This is probably not the place for argument. It may take several minutes, but once he winds down you can let him know you understand how strongly he feels, but you have a job to do anyway. If he fires up again, give him more time to vent, then start once more into the purpose of the meeting. Stay calm and speak more softly than your agitated employee. This may help him calm down over time. Don't rush things; he'll almost certainly exhaust himself eventually at which point you can proceed. Realize that, depending on what you have to say, he may fire-up all over again. If that happens, be prepared to repeat the previous steps to give him time to calm down. Then get back to the message you must deliver.

Don't back down when you know you're right. As you well know from your street experience, some people bluff and bluster for the purpose of backing down others and getting their way. Do not let an employee intimidate you. Be patient. Let him talk; let him vent. But do not acknowledge error or unfairness when you know that you are both correct and impartial. Stick by your guns without fail. Make it clear that you are doing so. Make direct eye contact with your employee. Speak clearly and plainly. Don't raise your voice, but don't whisper, either. If you have done your research well you have nothing to apologize for. Conduct the performance review session and be clear on where improvement is needed. Do not omit something you intended to say just because your subject is resistive or downright nasty. Do you job and don't allow either a whiner or a would-be bully to divert you from your purpose.

Own your work, rely on your courage. If what you have to say is unpopular, do not blame it on someone else. Own up to your fact-based opinions and do not hesitate to voice them as your own. Remember, your boss didn't do the evaluation, you did. Have the necessary courage to claim your work. You will lose the respect of your employees *and* your supervisor if you attempt to lay off unpopular opinions or findings on others. A leader doesn't do that. A leader tells the truth, not because he's cruel but because he's ethical and courageous.

Be prepared to take a break. If you sense emotions heating up it may be beneficial to take a ten-minute break to allow things to cool down. If you want, you can allow the employee to save face by saying that you need a bathroom break. Put some distance between the two of you for a few minutes and then get back on topic. Keep in mind that it's not necessary that your employee say he agrees with everything you have to say. State what you have to say and move on. You are, after all, attempting to communicate, not grind the person across the table into the dirt.

Keep your boss in the know. If you realize a performance review session did not go well it's a good idea to let your own supervisor know that, along with a few details about where the disagreement lies. He or she will be prepared if your employee seeks to appeal your views to a higher court. Once again, do not apologize for doing your job and telling the truth.

Follow-up as required. If your performance appraisal called for an employee to do or refrain from doing something, you will need to know that he accomplished the called for action. If he doesn't, further corrective or disciplinary action should follow. But you won't know what happened unless you check up. If your employee has in the meantime passed to another supervisor, that individual should be made aware of the call for specific action. Follow-up is an important part of every performance appraisal process. Do not allow it to be avoided or neglected.

PLANNING FOR THE FUTURE

The performance appraisal session has not terminated when you have reviewed your employee's past work. The next important task is to give the individual some worthwhile guidance regarding what should happen in the future. The goal is to build on exhibited strengths, shore up weaknesses, and help an employee further his or her career and job satisfaction wherever possible. The idea is to increase your subordinate's value to the organization while helping him get more personal positives out of what he is doing now and will do in the days and years to come.

It's always best if your employee agrees that the work goals you have set for him are worthwhile and need to be accomplished. For that reason it's preferred that he shares in their establishment. Ask him what he wants to accomplish during the next review period. He might do your objective-setting job for you. But realize that you may have to tone down unrealistic desires ("I want to go to the FBI National Academy right away" and gently insert the goals you know truly need accomplished "improve your spelling"). There is not a "magic" number of goals or objectives involved in the performance appraisal process. If you have set a complex, time-consuming task for your employee, that one goal may be enough. There is no specific limit on the number of shorter, simpler objectives that may be set, but half a dozen would be approaching the upper limit.

Problems or weaknesses identified during the appraisal process cry out for goals and objectives designed to "fix" them. If, for example, you have identified arrest control skills as a weak area for your employee, a goal to obtain additional training in those skills would be very appropriate for the next evaluation period. If your employee has had a problem with citizen complaints of discourtesy, then a goal seeking zero sustained beefs of that nature would be just the ticket.

Employee goal-setting should be regarded by everyone involved as just as important as every other part of the appraisal process. The employee should be recognized for meeting his goals. Action also needs to be taken if he fails to meet them without very good cause. That action can range from additional time to get them done to continuing them into the next review period to corrective discipline. The point is that an effective leader does not permit an employee goal he has established to be ignored by the individual he set it for. Performance goals and objectives are intended to help, not hinder or punish, the individual employee and his organization.

Used appropriately, work performance goals and objectives bring focus for both the law enforcement employee and his supervisor. They point in the direction of precisely what needs to get done. They emphasize what is considered important. They help get the job done. They are worth the effort that goes into their construction.

Establishing job performance goals and objectives for his subordinates is an integral part of a supervisor's responsibilities to his employees and his employer. By helping them establish performance targets for themselves, the leader can help his people improve their performance and, hopefully, expand their career opportunities within the agency. As the leader helps his charges get better at what they do, he simultaneously strengthens the organization of which they are all a part.

SUMMARY

No one said that the job of evaluating employee performance would be an easy one. To do it well the supervisor must be a careful observer, an impartial reporter, and a great communicator. He has to be able to be both honest and tactful in delivering his observations to his subordinate. He must be personally courageous enough to let his employee know where improvement is required and then hold him accountable to make those changes in his performance.

The leader also must let his charges know what they are doing well and praise them honestly for their good work. The leader does not offer false praise, as he knows it will be seen as insincere. He will do everything he can to support his employees as they go about doing their difficult jobs. Even as he evaluates he will be a cheerleader, too.

As an effective leader you realize the importance of an impartial and accurate performance review for employee and organization alike. You know that you have to be a clear and skillful writer and include plenty of clear examples of both positive and negative work in order to present an accurate record of your employee's performance. You realize that the performance review meeting with your employee is important and you guarantee that adequate time is available to do it right. You also get the review document done on time and ascertain that it is not a surprise to the recipient.

As a solid leader you likewise see to it that the performance review does not over-emphasize figures and quantity over accomplishment and quality. You keep your focus on outcome over output. That's what a leader does. That's what *you* do as you help your employee realize his or her full potential.

Chapter 8

HOW TO HANDLE COMPLAINTS
(WHEN THINGS GO WRONG)

The police services consumer who feels he or she has been mistreated or otherwise wronged by the law enforcement organization and its agents is a complainant. So is your fellow supervisor or manager who tells you with considerable animation that one of your charges has done wrong. Each of these people is unhappy about something. Each of them expects you to hear them out. And every one expects you, the law enforcement leader, to do something to set the situation right. Welcome to the role of law enforcement complaint receiver, mediator and fixer.

There are any number of ways in which you can find yourself thrust into the role of complaint processor. As an identifiable source of authority within your organization, it is just natural that people will turn to you to receive and resolve their problems. How you handle that role will reflect on you and the agency you represent. It also will help establish your reputation as an effective and caring leader, as well as a fair one. This chapter offers pointers on doing the job effectively and compassionately.

A CHANGE IN MIND-SET

You have heard repeatedly how your life will change when you become a first-line supervisor – a leader. You have been told that many of your on-the-job friends will treat you differently. You doubtlessly have been told that, especially now, you live in a glass house and must comport yourself accordingly. All of that is true. But what you may not have heard is how you will now be expected to regard gripes and complaints from the public and others.

As an officer you could scoff at the citizen complainers and dismiss their beefs as sour grapes. If you were cornered by a citizen wishing to complain about police misconduct – yours or somebody else's – you could pretty much wash your hands of the affair by summoning a supervisor to handle the complaint processing and schmoozing for you. But your world has now changed. Now, you *are* the supervisor. You *are* the grievance processor. Now it is you who must act, not someone else. And that's a big deal.

More yet is required of you before you can take the complaint and begin looking into exactly what happened. It is your whole attitude towards your citizen-complainant and what he or she has to say that must change. As a first-line officer you could, if you chose, dismiss all complaints against cops as lies from crooks and deranged people. Now, you must listen to them with an open mind. Now, in order to do your job well you must assume that what a perhaps-disagreeable individual is saying to you just *might* be the truth, or some shade of it. For many new supervisors, that requires a growth and maturation process. No one said it would be easy. Certainly you are capable of handling the shift in mind-set. But not all of your compatriots make the transition effectively.

Once upon a time in a really good law enforcement agency, a brand-new sergeant took a telephoned complaint from a verbally belligerent, intoxicated woman who claimed she had just been molested during a traffic stop by one of the supervisor's employees. The sergeant properly contacted the woman, but throughout the encounter approached the complainant as the nasty drunk he had met all too many times in his career as a first-line cop. He assumed she was lying in order to get an officer in trouble. His "I don't believe you, one of my people wouldn't do that" approach made an already uncooperative "victim" even more uncooperative and effectively destroyed the opportunity to collect physical evidence that may well have proven or disproven her tale. Justice was served for no one, as the local media was quick to announce. As it turned out, the accused officer had, in fact, done some things wrong. The department looked bad for its initial handling of the complaint. The rookie sergeant looked even worse.

RECEIVING GRIPES

You definitely do not want to stumble into the same pitfall that befell the young sergeant. You instead want to learn from his mistakes in order not to repeat them. A big piece of your mistake prevention effort can be found in how you receive a complaint in the first place, regardless of the source.

Your first responsibility is to retain an open mind, regardless of how far out or inaccurate you may believe the complaint to be at first blush. Your job is to get at the unvarnished truth, even if the complainer is someone who is loathsome to you. Loathsome bad guys sometimes have true stories of police maltreatment, too. It is up to you to be a good listener, not just because it's the right (and polite) thing to do, but because it will help you to find out what actually happened. A facial expression or body language that tells the speaker you do not like or believe him will make it hard to gather information. You need that information. If it turns out you are being lied to, that information (or misinformation, as it may be) can be used later to hold a dishonest complainant accountable for his dishonest deeds.

A veteran internal affairs sergeant at a medium-sized police department put it this way: "Before I took this assignment, I would hear something and say 'that's absolutely impossible.' After doing this job for a while, I don't say that anymore."

The point is that in order to be an impartial and effective complaint processor, you must be able to maintain an open mind until all of the facts are in, no matter how unlikely some of those details may seem at first blush. It's what you would do in a criminal investigation. You must hold yourself to the same high standard when the "suspect" happens to wear a badge. If the accused turns out to be absolutely innocent of the charges levied (as most often he or she will be), so much the better. But it is your responsibility to seek out the true facts without bias, fear or favor. That's what a leader does.

INVESTIGATING ALLEGATIONS OF WRONGDOING

Your job as a complaint processor will be made easier if your employer has sought to minimize legitimate complaints in the first place through solid problem prevention practices. Those practices start with careful hiring processes that include detailed background and psychological investigations of all applicants. Competent and comprehensive training can further reduce police behavior problems, as can ethical, alert and courageous supervision.

Misunderstandings and complaints will remain no matter how excellent the law enforcement organization and its people. That is when you will be called upon to hear the complainant out, ask a lot of questions, determine the real facts and help address any issues you find to exist.

Many law enforcement agencies differentiate in their handling of relatively minor allegations of employee misconduct as opposed to very serious allegations, such as complaints of criminal conduct. On the lighter end of the scale might be the allegation that an officer was rude to the complainant; the heavier end might see a complaint of sexual assault or robbery. The so-called minor complaint often will be received, investigated and adjudicated by the first-line supervisor. The serious allegation probably would be handled by the agency's internal affairs or professional standards unit. Even if the complaint is grave enough to be handled by a special unit, the first-line supervisor (you!) still should be involved in the final analysis of whether or not misconduct occurred and, if so, what to do about it.

You likely already know (or will soon figure out) that all kinds of people complain against police officers for all kinds of reasons, some legitimate and some not. The complainers can range from the housewife who feels she should have gotten a warning instead of a ticket to the ex-con who wants to "deal" by accusing his arresting officer of felony theft. You also know (or shortly will) that citizens' reasons for reporting police malpractice will range from the confused little old lady who honestly believes she was wronged, to the criminal who seeks revenge against the officer who captured him by constructing lies out of whole cloth. As a leader you will be asked to handle all of these – and more.

Law enforcement organizations investigate complaints against their personnel, policies and practices for several excellent reasons. The first is to protect the community from actual police malpractice. The second is to protect police employees from the effects of false or mistaken allegations. The third is to ferret out and fix erroneous or defective law enforcement policies and procedures. Yet another is to protect the reputation and credibility of the law enforcement agency. None of these goals would be accomplished if the agency simply permitted allegations to float around in a sort of never-never land without being honestly resolved.

Unless your agency is a very unusual one, most of the complaints made against its personnel will turn out to be unfounded, either the result of a lack of information, a misunderstanding or misinterpretation, or, occasionally, outright lies. Nevertheless, a lot of time, energy and effort must be expended in processing, investigating, and adjudicating them. You as a leader will need to be intimately involved.

A smart law enforcement organization will grant its first-line supervisors a great deal of discretion when it involves them in the complaint resolution process. Minor complaints should be almost entirely the responsibility of the first-line leader. Whether the situation is handled informally with no written record made or whether a form of some sort must be completed for documentation purposes will vary from one department to the next. Common sense and the mandate to keep paperwork to a minimum should both be considered here.

A traffic-related or discourtesy complaint could be seen as a good example of the sort of beef that might be handled informally by the first-line supervisor with a minimum of time and red tape. The supervisor receives the complaint or inquiry by telephone, text, e-mail or in-person and then re-contacts the reporting party to learn yet more details and answer his own questions about the incident. Courtesy and patience must be his bywords throughout the encounter. He may be able to answer the complaining party immediately by his own knowledge of the incident in question or relevant laws, policies and procedures. If not, he promises to get back to the citizen and then gathers the information he needs to better illuminate the situation. He reviews whatever documentation may be involved and then contacts the identified employee or employees to get "the rest of the story." (There will virtually always be another side.) Throughout the entire process the smart supervisor keeps in mind the need for fairness to all involved along with all the speed reasonable under the circumstances. Both the complaining party and the accused employee deserve a quick resolution to the conflict.

Just as in the criminal investigation, you often will find much value in the statements of any independent witnesses to the conduct complained of, whether they happen to be uninvolved police employees or, even better, citizens who just happened to be in the right place at the right time to see something. An area canvass for witnesses can be just as vital to the alleged police misconduct investigation as it is to the criminal case. A check for closed-circuit TV cameras that might have picked up the incident in question is worth the effort, too. Today's proliferation of these security devices has greatly increased the likelihood that somewhere a visual record of the happening just might exist.

Many times it will be possible to get the accused officer's side of events by simply asking him to write a memorandum or letter to you answering the important questions regarding what happened. In the case of a more serious accusation it may be necessary to do formal, taped interviews of all of those having information concerning what happened, including the accused officer(s). If there is even a remote chance that the officer's alleged conduct involved activity that was criminal in nature, then something called the *Garrity warning* comes into play. This all comes about because of a court case called *Garrity v. New Jersey.*

In *Garrity*, investigators interviewed several officers concerning their involvement in a ticket-fixing scheme. Before the interview, each officer was told that: anything he said could be used against him at trial; he had the right to refuse to answer a question if doing so would incriminate him; failure to answer questions would subject him to termination from employment. The officers were thus placed in the position of either answering the questions and possibly being prosecuted or refusing to answer and being fired.

Several officers answered the questions and were convicted. They appealed their criminal convictions on the grounds that they were coerced into answering by threat of termination. The Supreme Court agreed that the damning information given by the officers was indeed coerced or produced under duress.

Since *Garrity*, public employers including police agencies have realized that self-incriminating statements made by employees who were ordered to talk "on pain of discipline" during internal investigations or administrative inquiries cannot be used against those same employees during criminal proceedings. If an officer's conduct is the focus of both an administrative and a criminal investigation being carried out by separate investigators, while the criminal investigators can share what they learn with the administrative investigators, the same does not hold true for the administrative sleuths who have gained their knowledge from "coerced" responses from the employee. The key for the employee being interviewed is that he must answer *truthfully* to avoid additional repercussions.

What this means to you is that you must proceed cautiously to assure that all interests, including your employees', are protected and impartially served. Your wisest course of action if you even suspect that *Garrity* may be required is to seek guidance from your own supervisor, the department's attorney or legal advisor and/or your agency's internal affairs office before proceeding. There is most often no rush involved; it is far more important to do the job correctly. The interests of public, agency, and employee must be equally well-served.

Your agency likely will prefer that you give an employee his *Garrity* warning or advisement in written format and obtain his witnessed signature to indicate he has received it. That document will become a part of the file that details the investigation and its findings. While the advisement may vary a bit from one jurisdiction to the next, it generally looks something like this:

ADVISEMENT FOR INTERNAL AFFAIRS OR ADMINISTRATIVE INVESTIGATION INTERVIEW PURSUANT TO *GARRITY*

You are being questioned regarding an official investigation by the _____ Police Department. You will be asked questions specifically and narrowly related to the performance of your official duties or fitness for office, and your knowledge of pertinent events.

If you answer truthfully, neither your statements nor any information or evidence which is gained by reason of such statements can be used against you in any subsequent criminal proceeding. However, these statements may be used against you in a subsequent administrative personnel action.

If you answer untruthfully, your statements or any information or evidence which is gained by reason of such statements can be used against you in any subsequent criminal proceeding.

You are entitled to all the rights and privileges guaranteed by the laws and Constitution of this state and the Constitution of the United States, including the right not to be compelled to incriminate yourself. If you refuse to answer questions relating to the performance of your official duties or fitness for duty, you will be sub-

ject to administrative personnel action which will result in your termination from employment with the Police Department.

Interviewer _____ Date _____
Witness _____ Date _____
Employee _____ Date _____

Garrity is not something you will have to deal with on a frequent basis. Most of the complaints and inquiries you field will be of the plain
vanilla, "the cop was rude" or "I just don't get it" variety. Nonetheless,
by preparing yourself for handling the more serious allegation you will
be prepared for responding to the minor ones. By doing that you will
make yourself a more competent and caring complaint processor.

RESOLVING COMPLAINTS

Oftentimes you will find that your job as complaint processor has
morphed into the task of problem solver before your work is done. In
getting there you will need to carry out a bevy of separate, but related
and equally important actions. Having completed your inquiry into the
conduct complained about, as leader you must now examine the facts
and findings that your information gathering have brought to light.
Next, you must review the applicable rules, policies, procedures, orders, regulations and statutes impacting the situation at hand. You will
need to consider all of those pertinent guidelines in determining what,
if anything, was done wrong. Many law enforcement agencies catego-
rize the disposition of complaints in one of several ways:

Sustained – the alleged misconduct actually occurred.

Misconduct not based on complaint sustained – the employee
was not "guilty" of the accusation, but the investigation revealed some
other problem, either personnel- or procedure-related. For example,
the officer did not steal the complaining party's money, as alleged.
However, he did not follow proper procedures in logging or otherwise
handling the cash.

Unfounded – the alleged misconduct did not occur.

Exonerated – the employee did what he was accused of doing. However, doing so was exactly what he should have done under the circumstances. An example might be found in the officer accused by a parent of handcuffing her violent, intoxicated, teen-aged son.

Defective policy, procedure or practice – the accused employee was following the department's guidelines, but the directives themselves were faulty. Revision of the directives is required; no sanctions should be imposed against the employee.

Depending upon the seriousness of the infraction and your agency's way of doing things, you may make these findings alone or be part of a whole chain of command that looks at the facts and determines what to do next. (Note: your chain of command needs to be kept up-to-date during the entire time that you are looking into the complaint and reaching your findings.) Regardless, it is extremely important that you have a say in the process. Complaint resolution is one of the most important things that a law enforcement agency does. The involvement of its key, front-line leaders is mandatory.

Once the issue of the employee's "guilt" or "innocence" has been determined, both the employee and the complaining party must be notified without unnecessary delay. For the employee, oral notification followed up by a memorandum or letter is often the best way to go. For a complaining citizen, either a telephone call or a letter from the head of the organization will work, depending once again upon the seriousness of the allegation. For minor complaints, a contact from you, the first-line leader or mid-manager, will often be appropriate.

It is worth remembering that one or even both sides of the complaint may not be happy with your findings. The notification process is not the time to get into an argument over either the findings or the department's response. Endeavor to deliver the information in a tactful, calm, courteous manner and refuse to get drawn into an altercation. If there is a further appeal process, be sure the individual you are talking with is told how to pursue that avenue. Accept that there may be situations in which agreement is out of the question. Try to be satisfied knowing you have done your best and treated everyone involved with dignity and respect.

There yet remains the issue of responding effectively to actual misconduct by law enforcement. In other words, how do you fix it? Once more, the proper response will depend upon the gravity of the mistake. For the employee, the seriousness of the misstep, whether it was intentional or not, and his past disciplinary history will all factor into whether an oral warning or formal disciplinary action is required. Perhaps the answer is additional training. Or preventing a recurrence of the problem may require revision to an existing policy or procedure. Yet again, you as the most involved leader should have a big say in determining what is to be done with the "offender" as well as the "offense."

The complaining party needs to hear what the organization is doing to address the problem, too. A truthful explanation and sincere apology from you, a leader of the agency, may be all that is required to soothe ruffled feathers. Many citizens simply don't expect a government agency to ever admit it made a mistake. Hearing from you that it did and that it is actually sorry may disarm even the angriest complainer. (Just that response has worked many times before.) And while your agency has not authorized you to hand out sacks of money, if an error is within your ability to fix it, that is exactly the course of action you should follow. If, for instance, the department has mistakenly towed somebody's car, expediting the release of the vehicle from the "car jail" and paying the entire bill for the debacle would be the right thing for the police agency to do. Hopefully, you either have the authority to do that or can obtain it.

Dare to be innovative in solving a complainer's problem. Granted, words, no matter how sincerely meant, will not always do the trick. But it is always worth your efforts to try. You just might be surprised at your own success.

Finally, you must carefully document the entire saga from complaint reception to final disposition. Most agencies have a tracking system for complaints, so be sure you know how to use the one employed by your department. At the very least, a short memorandum should be created just in case the complaint and what was done with it ever surfaces again. Both the complainer and the one complained against deserve that clarity of record. Documentation dispels rumors of cover-up or preferential treatment given someone. Neither you nor your agency can afford to have those albatrosses left hanging around. Put them to rest through a complete and accurate record.

WHAT COMES NEXT?

It isn't likely that taking, investigating and adjudicating complaints from one source or another will become your favorite task as a law enforcement leader. It doesn't have to be. It will suffice that you are capable of carrying out these tasks when the situation demands it. By at least becoming relatively comfortable with the process you should be able to carry out your obligations to your organization, your community, and your employees.

As a leader you doubtlessly will have to carry out some of these tasks yourself. But familiarity with how they are to be done correctly should help you as you advance in the organization to the point where you are reviewing someone else's complaint processing work as opposed to doing it yourself. Knowing how to do it right will help you become a competent, well-rounded leader.

When you have received and investigated a grievance or complaint you have only partially completed the job. The next step calls for assuring that the needed correction or change, assuming one is necessary, actually gets made. If there has been an employee miscue that needs addressed, it will be your responsibility to assure that the task is carried out. If a broken policy or procedure resulted in a snafu, that problem will need solved, as well. If you are not the one correctly positioned in the organization to fix the situation, it will be your responsibility to assure that the need for the change is delivered to the attention of the individual(s) who actually can carry out the task.

You have probably had the frustrating experience of making a complaint to a government agency or private business and then suspecting that, empathetic and receptive words aside, your grievance was likely discarded as soon as you got off of the telephone. It is safe to assume that at least some of the complainants you encounter are making precisely the same, negative assumption about you and your organization. If the complaint has been established as a legitimate one, you owe the complainant more than nice words – and a brush-off. If you can fix it at your level, you are ethically obliged to do so. If not, get the concern where it can be handled. Once more, that's what a true leader does.

Finally, repairing a problem often requires more than a one-time, fix and forget strategy. A good leader also follows up to see if a once-repaired problem has actually stayed fixed. He is all too aware that on occasion a change in policy, procedure, or behavior, particularly a change that was unpopular when it was made, has a tendency to be forgotten when the boss is no longer looking. That is simply a not-too-admirable trait sometimes found in the human animal. Completing the job includes looking back on occasion to be sure that the task has really been finished.

SUMMARY

As a leader in your organization, people are going to seek you out when things go wrong. They are going to bend your ear when they feel that they have been mistreated, or are just plain unhappy. Sometimes they will just want to vent. Other times they will expect you to right a real or perceived wrong. And "they" can include your own employees and fellow supervisors as easily as members of the public. You are indeed everyone's complaint processor and "fix-it" specialist.

As you address the interests of police employees as well as police service consumers you maintain your own impartiality and sense of fair play. You serve as an open-minded, patient listener. You realize the importance of your role as the "person in the middle" and you strive to problem solve when it is possible to do so. When the issue has to be settled at another level, you do your best to pass the relevant information along with both accuracy and impartiality. You have learned from experience not to dismiss any complaint as "impossible."

You are mature enough to realize that you will never make everyone happy, and self-assured enough not to worry because you cannot. At the same time, you care enough to do your very best at complaint resolution no matter how disagreeable the complainant nor how serious (or frivolous) the complaint. You do it even when the police employee complained against is your friend. You are a leader and the task is among those that every effective leader must master. Indeed, you will.

Chapter 9

HOW TO FIX BROKEN BEHAVIOR

As the well-known bumper sticker will attest, sometimes "stuff" happens. It was not planned, it wasn't anticipated and it certainly wasn't welcome. But now, whatever the reason, there it is: a blemish on the otherwise handsome face of the law enforcement agency you work for and care about. As a leader of that agency, you should expect to have at least some responsibility for addressing the problem and removing the blemish.

Handling "stuff" that has gone wrong is one of your tasks as a law enforcement leader. How well you do it will help cast your reputation as a positive influence in your agency. At times something we term "discipline" will be required to mend the damage and, hopefully, prevent it from recurring. Discipline and its successful application will be the topic of this chapter.

Discipline is something you have heard cussed and discussed throughout your law enforcement career. Now you will have the opportunity to influence its definition and application in your law enforcement organization.

THE BEST KIND OF DISCIPLINE

You probably have heard *this* discussed throughout your career, also: the best kind of discipline is *self-discipline*, the discipline that comes from within. That sounds nice, but what, exactly, does it mean?

Self-discipline calls for someone – you, in this case – to want to do the right things for the right reasons, not because of fear of the possible

95

repercussions of being caught doing wrong. Self-discipline embodies the internal, personal rules and codes of conduct that you impose on yourself and then endeavor to follow scrupulously. Whether based on religious faith, an internal moral compass, a combination of the two or something else entirely, these codes drive you to do the proper thing because you think it is right, not because you fear punishment. Self-discipline says that you would do these things even if there was no one to watch you, no one who would ever know what you actually did under a given set of circumstances.

Self-discipline is something you display as a leader who desires to serve as an excellent role model for his or her people. It is something that you expect your subordinates to emulate. It is something that is found in quantity in a healthy organization.

A law enforcement organization well-supplied with employees who rely heavily on self-discipline for their direction is an organization that does not often have to rely on more coercive measures to gain employee compliance with the rules. There will always exist the need to mete out punishment for intentionally-committed, serious wrongs. The need for such measures simply will not arise often in an organization populated by personnel who practice self-discipline as their preferred means of guidance.

People who follow the rules except when there is an extremely compelling reason not to almost always display the self-discipline that helps make them solid law enforcement officers and leaders. You require that self-discipline to be a successful leader. It is an important part of the successful leader's character. It is a big part of what you are all about. Role-modeling self-discipline at all times will make it easier for your people to understand what you expect of them. Practicing that same self-discipline yourself will have the bonus value of denying anyone the opportunity to ever accuse you of maintaining a double standard.

WHY DISCIPLINE AT ALL?

There is a saying that all law enforcement supervisors should take to heart: "Ignore the bad ones, lose the good ones." It means just this: although they may never say so to your face, your employees often know who is doing his or her job properly – and who isn't. While they may never tell you so, they expect you to deal with the aberrant behavior.

If you send the message that you either cannot detect the bad behavior or (worse) you refuse for whatever reason to deal with it effectively, employees who DO care and ARE doing the job correctly will wonder why they are busting their hump when no one apparently cares. At the same time, they will lose whatever respect they may have had for you.

Your good employees always deserve your respect and support. Do not show them disrespect by failing to deal with substandard work or unethical, illegal or otherwise improper behavior by other employees. By intervening and correcting bad actions you also are doing the misbehaving employee a favor. You may be able to help him salvage his career before he gets in so deep that he cannot save himself. By helping redirect him you also are saving your employer (and your community) the time, trouble and money that would be spent in replacing the miscreant.

Everyone makes mistakes. Even you. Mistakes are inevitable. You are going to make some. So are your subordinates. Most mistakes are forgivable and retrievable. You learn things from making them. More than a few leaders have confessed that they learned more from past, painful missteps than from any other kind.

You likely know by now both from your life and leadership experiences that mistakes are of two kinds. The first category includes the "innocent" errors that people make simply because they didn't know any better or accidentally slipped up. These are the mistakes of the head that we all make. For cops, mistakes of the head can include forgetting to return an important phone call, booking a piece of evidence incorrectly or accidentally missing a scheduled court date. In the busy and complex world that your employees work in, mistakes of the head will happen. The key for you is not to become too wrought up over them. Oftentimes the urge to punish must be suppressed. At times talking works better.

The other (and more serious) kind of error is the *mistake of the heart.* In this situation the actor KNEW or should have known his chosen conduct was wrong, but did it anyway. Intent is generally involved here. These are not incidental or accidental occurrences. Sometimes they even involve planning and scheming before they are perpetrated. Oftentimes they include conduct that cannot be tolerated in an ethical law enforcement organization. Examples of mistakes of the heart could be lying to a supervisor about alleged misconduct, committing a crime such as stealing from a prisoner's property, or intentionally and repeatedly sleeping on duty. Like mistakes of the head, these kinds of errors are going to happen in every organization on occasion. When they do happen, prompt and firm organizational response is necessary. You always should be involved in helping determine that response if you happen to be the guilty party's supervisor.

Mistakes of the heart should be more heavily disciplined than mistakes of the head, which are most often "honest" errors. While a mistake of the head may merit no more than an oral warning and/or additional training, intentional "heart" errors may call for a suspension without pay or even termination.

Discipline is a great educator. That is another good reason for bothering to do it at all. You can learn a lot from the consequences of doing wrong. True, experiencing the consequences of bad behavior can help convince the offending employee that he shouldn't do that again. But the benefits of discipline extend far beyond the perpetrator of the misdeed. Corrective action for one actually educates all of the members of the organization who learn about it, as most will. Everyone learns what is and is not acceptable conduct. Everyone learns of the possible consequences of such behavior.

Every disciplinary action you take should be done with the understanding that the whole organization is watching. Members of the organization will have opinions about the fairness of what you are doing. That is another reason why it is vital that the discipline you dish out is both appropriate and fair.

All discipline has a powerful ability to teach. It can prevent misconduct as well as correcting it. As a leader in your organization you are responsible for assuring that what is taught is precisely what you want your subordinates to learn.

As noted already, it is important that you as a supervisor participate in disciplinary decisions involving your employees. If you have been as involved with your employees as you should be, you will be familiar with the offending employee's personality strengths, weaknesses, work and discipline history. Having you closely involved should help assure that the discipline selected is just and appropriate for the employee. After all, you as his supervisor should know him better than anyone else in the chain of command.

Keeping you, the supervisor, involved in disciplinary decisions personalizes it for the recipient. "Overkill" can be avoided, just as letting the previously-offending employee off too easily can be dodged, as well. Finally, being intimately involved in the process can strengthen you as a leader. You learn a lot. Perhaps more important, your subordinates are shown evidence of your importance as a leader whose opinions are valued by the Top Brass. Those same subordinates may be more likely to pay heed to your directions, guidance, requests and warnings in the future.

HOW TO DISCIPLINE EFFECTIVELY

To be effective, discipline must be timely, fair and appropriate for the infraction committed. It can be neither too harsh nor too lenient. It should not be administered until all the facts are in and it is clear that corrective action is warranted, but it certainly should not be delayed any longer than that. Having all the facts at hand means that the accused employee has had the opportunity to tell his side of the story, to include any mitigating circumstances that you as the disciplinary authority need to know.

Disciplinary discussions need to be carried out privately. Only you and your employee should be present. You must avoid leaving the impression that the employee is being ganged-up on. At the same time, uninvolved peers of the employee or other passersby have no business witnessing the discussion, either.

Discipline, in order to be perceived by the recipient as fair, must be consistent with what has happened before under similar circumstances. Assuming the disciplinary history of the two employees is identical or very similar, the discipline Employee B receives should be the same as Employee A garnered for the same violation of the rules. This is often referred to as *comparative discipline.* Police unions and attorneys representing police employees during disciplinary appeals will look for this indication of fairness. It is also the right thing to do.

The concept of *progressive discipline* also comes into play here. This simply means that the idea of "start light, get heavier as required" is appropriate in discipline. For example, a first missed court appearance might draw an oral warning, a second a letter of reprimand, and a third a suspension without pay. The intended message is "you didn't get it the first time so now I'm going to do something more to get your attention." That's appropriate, assuming there are no extenuating circumstances, such as a really good excuse for the most recent infraction.

But those facts you already have learned from your information gathering. Certainly you can lighten (or increase) the level of correction as the facts dictate.

It's important that you have the authority to respond to the unusual situation as opposed to following a scripted list for disciplinary responses. If the facts clearly dictate departure from the scale, you must be able to tailor the corrective action to the specific situation at hand. When doing so, you must be able to clearly explain the reason for your out-of-line decision, both to your boss and the disciplined subordinate. If you have thought the situation through as clearly as you should have, that will not be problem for you.

Remember that you do not have to make tough disciplinary calls alone. Ask your fellow leaders for their advice. Your boss should be willing to give you his or her opinion, as well. You should make it clear when you are talking to all of these people that you are not asking them to make the decision for you. You are instead pulling on their knowledge of leadership as well as their recollection of what has gone before – organizational history, in other words – to apply to the present situation. The decision remains yours to make once you have completed your fact-gathering mission.

A word about your "final" disciplinary decision, however: be sure you have your organization's blessing before you notify your employee of the action contemplated. Whether that requires a formal written process or simply your immediate boss's OK will vary from organization to organization and from one level of discipline to another. Just be sure you are not placed in the position of having to "recall" discipline once it has been administered.

At the same time, realize that your agency's chain of command may alter discipline that you have arrived at in good faith, either via a disciplinary appeal process or other means. That happens sometimes, often for good reason. It does not mean you messed anything up. The Big Boss who changed the discipline may have had access to new facts you did not have. (It is absolutely alright for you to ask the person in the know for the reason for the change.) Just recognize that you did the right thing with the information you had and go on with life. There likely will be another disciplinary call awaiting you just down the road. Be prepared to make it without hesitating.

There is yet something more that discipline must be in order to be effective. It must be *documented.* For all practical purposes, discipline that did not get recorded in some manner did not happen. It cannot be used to influence employee performance appraisals or future disciplinary actions where more serious corrective measures are needed. It cannot be used because, officially, it does not exist.

All too often well-meaning supervisors give an employee a break for a "first offense" by not in any way recording the miscue and the corrective action taken via a supervisory log entry, computer record or other means for memorializing positive and negative employee performance. Then, the employee moves along to a second supervisor who, six months or a year later, observes the same misbehavior. He checks for a record of previous, similar actions, finds none, and gives the employee another break because it's a "first offense." And so on into the future. In this state of affairs it is possible for an employee needing additional supervisory intervention to go for a long time – perhaps a dangerously long time – without receiving it. That's bad for employee and employer alike. And the whole sad scenario started with a failure to document bad behavior and what was done to fix it. Record performance problems and what you did to address them. It may save many people (including you) a lot of grief in the future.

It is desirable that the employee receiving disciplinary action understand why he is receiving it and accept the correction as just. That is the ideal state of affairs, and sometimes things work out exactly that way. But realize that not every employee you discipline is going to accept what you do and say as valid. In fact, he or she may be downright vocal about the miscarriage of justice he feels you are perpetrating. It is important to let an unhappy employee vent, at least to a point. You can try taking a different tack to explain the situation. Be patient. Try to avoid a massive display of authority ("Because I said so, that's why!") Be empathetic. But realize that in the end you may occasionally have to end the exchange with an agreement to disagree. That's life. Try not to hold a grudge, even though your employee may. There's too much else to do to spend time dwelling endlessly on something that is past. Hopefully your employee eventually will come to the same place. If not, put it behind you and move on.

It is worth saying one more time: try to know your employee as well as reasonably possible when imposing corrective action. By doing so you may be able to anticipate how he will react to correction and thereby be prepared for a thoughtful response. One employee may be angered and insulted while another may be embarrassed and hurt. If you have an idea of what to expect you can better plan your approach. Praise his or her strengths and good work too, if appropriate under the circumstances. Knowing your employee well also should help you tailor the discipline to the "offense." This may aid you in determining when formal action versus an oral "don't do that again" is appropriate. As you know, effective discipline should be carefully tailored, not mass produced.

YOUR JOB AS COUNSELOR

Sometimes you may find your responsibilities as disciplinarian and employee counselor to be closely related. On occasion you may find that simply advising a subordinate to avoid behavior that got him into trouble in the first place may be all that is needed to assure that the problem does not recur. Counseling also can provide an employee with advice on how to stay out of trouble entirely. And in yet other situations counseling advice proffered by a caring supervisor (you!) may cover territory entirely unrelated to discipline yet extremely valuable to the employee – assuming he or she is paying attention to what you have to say.

Sometimes it will be obvious that your counseling assistance is needed. The employee who is chronically late to work for no apparent good reason clearly is in need of your investigatory attention and counseling advice. But many other work world situations will not be nearly so clear-cut. An example may be found in the officer who "just isn't acting like himself anymore," but is not exhibiting any other obvious signs that something is amiss.

But before the leader can help his employee through whatever difficulty he is facing he must recognize that a problem exists. Everyone is, of course, different and each individual reacts at least somewhat differently to abnormal stress. Nevertheless, there are some generally agreed upon signs of pending or already developed trouble. The alert leader who detects the presence of one or more of them should be aware that his intervention may be needed. These warning flags of a troubled employee often include the following:

- A normally talkative and outgoing employee becomes quiet and withdrawn

- A punctual and reliable employee begins arriving to work late, or not at all
- The employee displays indications of alcohol or drug abuse
- The employee's work performance deteriorates markedly
- The officer accumulates a steady tally of employee misconduct complaints
- The officer's use of force incidents increase noticeably in number
- The employee displays frequent fits of anger in the workplace when he/she did not previously do so
- Peers complain that the employee is not "carrying his share of the load"
- A formerly reliable employee begins dodging calls or other work assignments
- A normally well-groomed and attired employee begins coming to work poorly groomed or with soiled/disheveled clothing.

Other indicators of problems can exist, of course. Whatever constitutes unusual behavior for a particular individual may spell trouble – and call for the responsible leader to inquire further.

Once a problem has been recognized, it is likely that a supervisory response is indicated. But exactly what should be done, and how?

In a best-case scenario the afflicted employee will approach his boss – you, in this case – and calmly lay out the particulars of what is troubling him. Things may, in fact, work out that way. At least as often, however, the leader must inquire gently, probe softly and otherwise seek to determine what is really bothering his subordinate. That, too, is part of your job description.

The list of possible maladies that could be plaguing your employee is practically endless. Potential problems can range from marital difficulties to trouble adjusting to a new work schedule or car partner. They can run the problem spectrum from workplace conflicts to alcoholism or prescription drug abuse. It will be up to you to ferret out the trouble and, hopefully, start your subordinate on the road to troubleshooting it. Note that it will remain the employee's task to fix the problem, not yours. You can offer advice, guidance and suggestions. You cannot and should not solve someone else's problem for him.

Particularly if your charge is reluctant to bring you into his confidence, you may need to depend on alternative sources to gather the information you will need in order to help. Personnel files and earlier performance review documents may contain a wealth of relevant information. So can employee logs and disciplinary records. (This may not be the first time a significant problem has reared its head.)

The affected employee's peers may know quite a bit about what is going on, but you should be cautious in approaching them. You should make it clear that you are not trying to get them to "tattle" on their colleague. Sometimes a "I wonder what's bothering Susie and how we could help her?" may be the best approach. But be careful not to press a fellow employee too hard, as some employees may be afraid and reluctant to talk about a fellow officer, even for the purpose of helping him. Worse from your standpoint, a grilled employee may rush to tell his pal that the boss is checking up on him.

Your sit-down with your employee likely will demand all of your abilities as a leader who is sincerely interested in the welfare of his employee. Exceptional listening skills will be required, as will your knack for displaying patience and tact. You will listen carefully to everything your employee has to say, even if you suspect that you've heard it all (or something very similar) before. Patient and attentive listening requires that you do not interrupt unnecessarily. You also should maintain good eye contact and give occasional, encouraging head nods to indicate that you are listening and understand. An open, relaxed posture on your part also may help to calm an excited employee who may now start to realize that he is not going to be attacked.

Privacy and quiet are musts for the spot where the two of you sit down to talk. An avoidance of interruptions is important, too. Meanwhile, it is important that you steer clear of pronouncements, judgments or expressions that betray shock or disapproval on your part. Try to keep an open mind about what your subordinate has to say. It is only human to have some preconceived notions about what the person has to say, or what you *think* he is going to say. It's when these ideas and feelings interfere with your impartiality and good judgment that they can cause you problems.

While you want to avoid interrupting your employee unnecessarily, be prepared to bring him back to the subject at hand – his tardiness or whatever – if he strays too far afield. This is not the time to allow your employee to deploy every excuse or grievance that has occurred to him since Noah's flood. Focus is important in problem solving.

A word about a counseled employee's right to privacy: it is up to the employee and not his boss if he wants to make his trials and tribulations known to his compatriots. You should not share with them what he said, did, or complained about. A leader who unnecessarily betrays his employees' crises and confidences to others is a leader in whom subordinates eventually will lose trust. If that happens you will find that your value to your employees and your employer is much reduced.

Know that you are not a professional counselor and are not properly equipped for an in-depth counseling role. The good news is that there are plenty of folks out there with the requisite education and a desire to help. Once you get an idea of what your charge's difficulties seem to be you can refer him to some sources of skilled, professional help. Your employer may have an Employee Assistance Program. You may be able to call upon the expertise of your Human Resources Department, or an outside counseling and support workhorse such as Alcoholics Anonymous. There are lots of legitimate experts out there eager to help a troubled soul. Point your employee in the right direction and leave the follow-up to him. He is more likely to be supportive of the effort if he makes the contact himself.

Even as you labor in earnest to aid a troubled employee, keep in mind the "prime directive" for employee counselors everywhere: Do everything reasonable to help. Be honest, patient, helpful, empathetic and supportive in your efforts. But remember that you did not cause your employee's problems nor are they your own. You can and should provide emotional support and sage advice. But you cannot solve your subordinate's problems for him. That's his job. Be content that you helped set him on the right path to do so.

SPINE WANTED, INQUIRE WITHIN

Human beings tend to put off things that they don't enjoy doing. They tend to delay doing things that they feel others will find unpleasant. As a consequence, many supervisors will put off making disciplinary decisions and taking disciplinary actions. You might even confess to having such a tendency yourself.

Disciplinary decisions that are unnecessarily delayed help no one. The same holds true for the carrying out of disciplinary actions. This game of "kick the can down the road" harms everyone, most especially the intended recipient of the discipline. Basic human psychology says you don't give junior a time-out today for pulling his little sister's hair a month ago. Understandably, he is unlikely to make a connection between his bad actions and the negative consequences. It works the same way with adults. In addition, an individual's recollection (or interpretation) of what he did can change over time. The more that time passes, the more his mind may practice "revisionist history" to the point that he no longer recalls that he did anything wrong.

To ensure fair treatment of everyone involved, your employee needs to know as soon as possible whether or not his boss feels he did wrong, and what his boss (that's you!) plans to do about it. If the miscue drew a lot of attention throughout the agency, many other people will want to know the final outcome, too. Knowing that will help them learn what they want to do – or avoid doing – in the future. Everyone expects, and rightfully so, that the drama will not be allowed to drag on endlessly. That is especially true for the employee accused of wrongdoing. Indeed, he might argue truthfully that he was a victim of "cruel and unusual punishment" if the matter is allowed to simmer for too long.

The solution to all of this? Get the discipline decided and done as quickly as reasonably possible. Delay benefits no one. Have the backbone to get unpleasant work done now so that everyone can move ahead. It is the right thing to do on every level.

You already know that having enough spine to carry out the difficult and otherwise unpleasant tasks is one of the things you must master if you are to be an effective leader. Having backbone enough to discipline appropriately someone who may have been (or still be) your pal is a requirement for a leader. Delaying the discipline will not make the task of levying it any easier. Your wisest course of action is to get it done now and move ahead. You may not gain the affection of the individual disciplined or that of his close buddies. But you well may gain their grudging respect as a leader who says what he means and means what he says.

As a leader you must always put your peoples' respect ahead of your need for their affection. You owe them as well as your organization that much. You can bet that your subordinates as well as your bosses will be assessing your spine quotient on a continuing basis. Never running from your duties as a disciplinarian will help convince all observers of your competency and courage as a leader. It also will make you feel better about yourself and your abilities.

SUMMARY

You now know a lot about discipline in the modern law enforcement organization. You know that how you handle the discipline of your personnel will have much to do with establishing your earned reputation for credibility and impartiality. You know that you must be a role model for your subordinates in the way you administer discipline. You realize that not dealing promptly and firmly with problem employees will cost you the support and good will of the good ones.

You are well aware that the best discipline is always self-discipline – the drive to do the right thing that comes from within. You also know that the errors you may have to correct are of two types: mistakes of the head and mistakes of the heart. You know that the mistakes of the head, or simply making an honest error, often can be corrected without punishment. Mistakes of the heart – misconduct by an employee who knew better – merit a more severe response. Additionally, you are keenly aware that discipline should not be delayed unnecessarily or it loses its intended effect. Likewise you recognize that discipline for one member of the organization can serve as education for all if it is properly handled.

You are not expected to enjoy disciplining your subordinates. At the same time, you recognize the value to the organization of discipline that is decisively, promptly and fairly administered. Discipline is not a bad thing.

As you face making disciplinary decisions you should remember that your peers in your organization's leadership ranks are there to assist you on the difficult calls. Do not hesitate to call on them for help. Naturally, you will offer yours in return. You also must avoid the temptation to put off administering corrective action when it is needed. You must resist the temptation to water down your disciplinary action just to placate an unhappy subordinate and/or his colleagues. Staying the course is as important in matters of discipline as it is in the other difficult challenges you face.

Chapter 10

HOW TO KEEP YOUR PEOPLE SAFE

Your goal as a safety-smart law enforcement leader should be to build a team of survival conscious officers around you. When your subordinates are as conscious of the need for safety on the job as you are, you will have succeeded in doing everything possible to keep your people safe. In reality, of course, the task will be never-ending. As your experience as a risk manager has taught you, there always will be one more thing you can do to help assure that your officers go home safely to their loved ones at end of watch.

Keeping your people safe will call on you to be an excellent role model who sets a good example for safety and survival at every opportunity. It will require you to be a safety teacher, inspector, advocate, counselor, and, occasionally, disciplinarian who corrects patently unsafe behavior. It will require you to be on your best game at all times lest you miss something that could have a negative, even disastrous impact upon the welfare of one or more of your charges.

Every law enforcement leader dreads the dark day when one of his or her people will come to serious harm because of a bad guy or because of the officer's own temporary inattention or carelessness. Every responsible leader strives to do his best to see to it that such a day never comes. At the same time, his own emotional survival requires that the leader recognize that he can only do so much. The rest remains in the hands of the employees he has trained and mentored. The exceptional leader does his utmost to bullet-proof his people, just as he seeks to help them in every other aspect of their very difficult job. This chapter will help him in the incredibly important effort to do just that.

109

WHAT'S TO WORRY ABOUT?

Quite a lot, unfortunately. There are the dangers that come with dealing with drunks, crazy people, bar fighters and felons of all stripes. Then there are the risks that accompany the many vehicle- and traffic-related tasks handled by your officers. They must handle reckless and intoxicated and senile motorists in addition to the "routine" risks of piloting a police car while keeping track of the vehicle's various electronics and scanning the vicinity for bad guys, all at the same time. Mix in the very real dangers of high-speed pursuits and high-risk vehicle stops and you have a virtual witch's brew of potential, traffic-related disasters.

Today's law enforcement training is of necessity more realistic than ever in helping prepare cops to face the hazards of the street. In order to survive on the job, officers need to ground fight, engage in use of force exercises against each other and train to defeat weapon takeaway attempts. On top of all that your people also take part in some real-world scenario firearms training. All of these training efforts are necessary and important. But officers are hurt and occasionally killed in training to survive. If this realistic training is not led by highly skilled and competent professionals it poses a major threat to the welfare of your personnel. Seeing that it is done right is yet another obligation you must shoulder as a leader.

Outdated or unsafe equipment is one more threat to your peoples' safety that you will need to watch out for as a leader. Old, abused and unreliable firearms and conducted energy devices are among the items that can get your people hurt if they fail to function as intended. They represent examples of the equipment issues you will face and fix as a good boss.

It is not enough that your officers survive the risks of the road in a physical sense, as important as that is. They also must maintain their emotional health and mental stability as they deal with a steady diet of the worst situations and the sorriest people the job can throw at them. Worrying about your subordinates' health in the emotional well-being department is one of your leadership responsibilities, too. This is one more important facet of your job that you cannot afford to neglect.

You also must be concerned about your agency's officer safety culture, or lack of same. If the organizational culture tolerates careless, reckless or otherwise "cowboy" behavior by sworn personnel, trouble is inevitably just around the corner. If someone has not been hurt (or worse) already, a personal tragedy is almost certainly coming. If foolhardy behavior is tolerated or even rewarded instead of being corrected, blue blood surely will flow sooner or later. You as a leader must do more than worry about a culture that allows or even encourages this kind of dangerous and irresponsible conduct. You are ethically bound to do your level best to change it. That may be no small task in a hidebound organization. It's one that nevertheless must be mastered.

In addition, it is your job as a leader to help assure that the officers under your command do not commit any of the fatal errors that have led to the death and injury of peace officers ever since something called law enforcement has existed. Only the close scrutiny of your agency's field operations and practices by interested and involved leaders will prevent the kind of deadly errors that can claim the life of a law enforcement officer. Those time-worn fatal errors include:

- False courage ("cowboy" or "cowgirl" policing)
- Poor approach or positioning at a call or contact
- Failure to wear body armor
- No use or improper use of back-up help
- No use or improper use of cover
- Improper handcuffing, including failure to handcuff
- Improper subject search, including no search at all
- Poor weapon retention practices
- Lack of proper training with equipment and tactics
- Risky assumptions; taking for granted things that are not known for a certainty
- Failure to remain constantly alert; general carelessness or complacency
- Failure to watch a suspect's hands
- Missing the danger signs (Example: a bulge in clothing that could be a weapon).

As you know all too well, honest mistakes by good cops can result in irretrievable tragedies. So can intentional shortcuts by careless or lazy officers. As a leader you will labor without end to nip unsafe practices in the bud and guide your people back to doing things the *right* way. You may well save a life in the midst of your endeavors.

REMEMBERING THE BASICS

As long experience has taught you, there are no shortcuts for staying alive on streets than can turn deadly without warning. When it comes to officer safety, taking a shortcut, cheating on "the rules," can get you killed.

There really is nothing fancy or complex about "the rules" for surviving the street. Safety-smart cops have been practicing them for a very long time. These guidelines for staying alive often amount to little more than common sense based on training, experience and good judgment. But as the officer fatality statistics show every year, too many cops still break these very basic rules. Some of them get lucky and nothing bad happens. But for the others whose luck has run out, a violent death can be the outcome of rule-breaking.

It will be your job as a leader to assure that your people know the rules. Even more important, you will see to the best of your ability that they follow them. This you will accomplish by observing the safety practices your people display on the job. Where you find skills lacking you will intervene to ensure that immediate corrections are made. Officer safety is too important to be left to "later on."

Keep in mind that as a leader you will get what you *inspect*, not necessarily what you *expect*. Checking up on what is being done on the job is yet another of your key responsibilities as a leader. At the same time, helping fix safety deficiencies should bring you great satisfaction as a leader. After all, what could be more rewarding than helping your people go home at the end of their shift without holes in their bodies that nature did not put there?

Before your people can follow the rules they have to know what they are. As noted, they do not involve rocket science or brain surgery. But they do require careful adherence to some basic, common sense guidelines intended to keep their practitioner safe. They include the following time- and experience-proven advice:

Never get complacent about the job. Carelessness kills cops. It is as simple as that. Not caring is worse than not knowing. Sleepwalking your way through your potentially dangerous job could put you to sleep permanently. Stay alert and stay alive.

Realize that there are off-duty dangers too. You can encounter danger even when off the job. It is important to know how (and if) to respond to an off-duty threat when you do not have some of the advantages that you do when you're working. Realize that on-duty cops responding to help you may not know you from a bad guy.

Don't try to be a hero. You don't need to work at being a hero. Chances are that sometime during a long and contributing career it'll happen anyhow. Don't go looking for the opportunity. Recognize that sometimes hero medals are given to their surviving relatives.

Never stop learning your job. Your job is constantly changing, just as is the environment you work in. Keep up your training and stay abreast of the updated survival material available to you through books, videos and the Internet. Talk to others. Learning is yet one more job that is never done.

Wear your body armor. If you work the street as a peace officer today you absolutely must wear it, and wear it properly. Body armor has saved thousands of law enforcement officers from death or serious injury as a result of both felonious assaults and accidents. Wear it without fail.

Do some contingency planning. During duty downtime, devote some mental effort towards determining what you would do to counter specific threat situations. There is evidence that officers who have thought through such scenarios in advance are more likely to win a similar confrontation when it occurs for real. Exercise your imagination.

Rely on your good common sense. If the hair on the back of your neck stands up and a little voice in your head says "don't do it," then don't. Rely on your life and job experience melded with your training and good judgment to keep you out of trouble. That's what common sense is really all about. Heed the little voice.

Never stop looking for the next threat. If you locate and neutralize one offender, keep looking for his partner(s). He may not be alone. If you find one weapon in a prisoner search, start looking for the next one and the next. Threats sometimes come in multiples. Never relax until all of the danger has passed.

Stay proficient with equipment and tactics. That fancy firearm is just an expensive paperweight if you cannot hit anything with it. The same principle applies to all the rest of your equipment. Practice really does make perfect, or close to it. Practice your field survival tactics and procedures, too, ranging from handcuffing to use of cover.

Stay in shape, both physically and mentally. A badly out of shape cop has a greater chance of losing a fight for his life. Stay healthy and physically fit and improve your chances of winning a potential fight to the death. Always maintaining a winning, "I'll never give up" mind-set can save your life, too. Take care of your body and mind and both will take care of you.

Don't make dangerous assumptions. Don't take anything as fact that you do not know for a proven certainty. Alarms are not always false. Bad guys aren't always gone by the time you arrive. And the fact that Blinky the Drunk didn't fight you the last five times you collared him doesn't mean he won't try to disembowel you this time.

Make the best possible use of solid cover. Train yourself to approach every call or contact with an eye towards where you could go for bullet-stopping protection if things go to Hell. Cover is relative; you want the best and the most solid that you can get behind very quickly.

Use back-up help wisely. Always call for a cover officer when you even *think* you will need one. And use your back-up helper wisely. Practice contact and cover tactics where one officer carries out the primary business of the contact while the other serves as his lifeguard (cover) – and nothing more. Get as much cover help as you need – it doesn't have to stop with one officer.

Watch your approach and positioning. Approach the call or contact using cover to your advantage. At night, keep your subject in the light and you in the dark to the extent feasible. But don't get too close too soon and set yourself up for a sudden attack. Be conscious of your position in relation to everyone else's at all times. Keep your threats in front of you.

Do not underestimate your opponent. True, some crooks are dummies. But your opponent also may be as good at his job as you are at yours. Respect his abilities. Never give him an opening to take advantage of. Until proven otherwise, assume that he knows what he's doing and will try to take you out.

Avoid being sleepy or asleep on the job. Sleepy or daydreaming cops make easy targets for bad guys. Get enough rest on your own time in order to be ready for anything the job throws at you. You'll stay healthier in more ways than one.

Keep watching your subject's hands. Chances are it's your opponent's hands or what he puts in them that will be the most likely to do you harm. Never lose track of his hands and tell him to keep them in your sight. Be prepared for a surprise to appear in one of them at any time.

Look out for the danger signs. There are lots of warning flags that a subject is planning to do you harm. Intoxication in your subject is a danger sign. So is irrational or delusional behavior. Ditto for unexplained nervousness or outright hostility. A bulge in clothing may indicate the presence of a hidden weapon. There are many more hazard warnings to watch for. Learn them and remain constantly alert for their presence. Change your tactical response when you suspect danger.

Maintain a "reactionary gap" between you and the party you are contacting. Keep a subject you are contacting at least six to ten feet away from you to give yourself time to react if he launches a sudden attack. When you do have to move in to handcuff and search, do both the right way and under the close watch of a cover officer. Do both with your subject off-balance and at a physical disadvantage.

Practice excellent weapon retention. Keep your weapons secure and positioned away from the quick grab of an offender. Practice the skill required to defend against and defeat an actual weapon grab attempt if it occurs. If it happens for real, remember that you are fighting for your life and all the rules of "polite" combat are out the window.

Critique your own safety practices and ask for others' observations, too. Look at your safety-related behavior on a regular basis. Ask yourself "Could somebody have had me today?" Resolve to fix any shortcomings you detect. It's perfectly acceptable to ask those you work with for their constructive criticism, too.

Survive mentally and emotionally, too. Surviving physically is half the job. Staying well in your head is vital, too. Don't bottle up things that are tormenting you. Always have someone to talk with about your fears, frustrations and innermost worries. Offer the same, nonjudgmental ear to someone else. That way everyone can come through whole. Never be reluctant to seek professional assistance if you need it. You may save your own life in the process.

Ask your people questions to gauge their grasp of these guidelines. Observe them regularly. See what they actually do on the job. But be prepared to revise your safety advice as the threats on the street and law enforcement's response to them change. New weapons and tactics in the hands of the bad guys will require a quick adaptation by law enforcement. Don't let yourself and your people be found wanting, since survival tactics and techniques change with the times. Keep up with current events and safety training in your profession to be sure you know what the new threats are and how to counter them. Stay abreast of the latest safety training that may benefit your employees. That, too, is one of the basics.

YOUR OBLIGATIONS TO YOUR PEOPLE

When it comes to officer safety and survival, as a leader you owe your subordinates a number of things. All of them have to do with your overarching effort to keep them physically and emotionally healthy as they go about doing a difficult job. Your obligations include the following:

You are obligated to be a positive role model. To put it succinctly, you must always serve as a good role model for your people regarding their safety and survival practices in the field. You must show them by example how you want the job done in order that they can go home intact at the end of their shift. In other words, you must always do it right if you expect them to do it right. More about that later.

You should be a skilled and tireless trainer. You should be assessing the training needs of your subordinates on a continuing basis. That is especially important in the area of officer safety. Your training needs surveillance efforts should include your graybeard officers as well as the fresh from the academy rookies. Bad safety habits can get ingrained over time and can only be fixed through the intervention of an interested (and relentless) supervisor.

Once you determine what your people need it will be up to you to provide what you are qualified to furnish and obtain elsewhere what you don't feel comfortable doing yourself. The skills an individual or your whole team requires may be found within your organization, or you may have to look outside for what you need. Regardless, it is up to you to point your people in the right direction and check to be sure they get there.

Training needs will change as the real-life threats and appropriate threat responses change, too. New safety equipment may require new skills and revised tactics. Stay on top of all these things and see that your people are briefed and educated accordingly. In doing so you will enable them to stay prepared for the challenges of the street.

You must be an always alert and devoted inspector and "fixer." As every veteran police supervisor knows, obtaining the behavior you want from your subordinates means being involved and engaged enough to see that it's being done the right way. It requires some energy and effort on the part of the supervisor. Especially where officer safety is concerned, the expenditure is clearly worth it.

The leader's inspection duties include equipment as well as employee performance. The employee will have difficulty doing it right if he does not have the equipment he needs. The equipment must be appropriate for the task and function properly, whether it is a police vehicle or a firearm. The employee likewise will have to demonstrate that he knows how to do the job once he is properly equipped for it. As a responsible leader you'll be watching to see if he knows what he's doing or needs a bit of help.

A leader accomplishes his inspection duties by getting out in the field where his employees actually do their work. (There are not that many safety-related things he can inspect while sitting behind a desk.) He looks at real-world operations, including traffic stops, arrests, prisoner searches, verbal de-escalation techniques and a myriad of other safety-related activities. He endeavors not to "hover" or get in the way, but he does stay involved and interested. He lets his people know that he is honestly concerned about their welfare and will be dropping by from time to time. That way they should not be surprised by his arrival.

Once he identifies safety shortcomings in his employees (or in the tools and tactics they have to work with), the leader takes effective action to remedy the problems he finds. He does not expect someone else to solve the problem for him. Nor does he put off addressing it until a later time. Safety is too important to be sidetracked.

You have an obligation to intervene as an effective risk manager, as necessary. In addition to all your other duties you are a risk manager for your agency. Your tasks here are closely related to those you handled as an inspector and "fixer." You, along with the other leaders in your organization, are responsible for saving both lives and dollars by preventing or correcting unwise and/or unsafe practices and behavior. It is both the humane and the financially responsible thing to do. Preventing accidents and losses of all kinds keeps employees safe while simultaneously saving money for your employer.

Detecting "risky" behavior by employees or ferreting out unsafe practices by the organization is only the first part of your job. You are also required to see that the problems, whether with personnel, policies, procedures or equipment are corrected right away. You and your organization cannot afford people, practices or things that are dangerous. If you wait until a disaster occurs before you attend to the problem, you have waited too long. Intervene now and avoid both the suffering and financial loss that your people and your organization cannot afford. Good risk managers do that all the time.

You are responsible to serve as a fearless advocate for your people and what they need in order to do their job safely and well. Sometimes being an advocate for your people's safety needs means lobbying your boss and the organization for needed equipment. Sometimes it translates into changing organizational policies, procedures or tactics that are unsafe, or at least not as safety sound as they should be. On occasion it may mean seeking more personnel for an understaffed team or watch. And yet other times it may require seeking additional training for employees you have found lacking in the safety basics. Whatever the case, speaking up at the right time and place in order to seek redress for real safety problems is your ethical responsibility.

Your knack for organizational survival and your understanding of organizational politics hopefully have taught you by now that you do not help your people by shouting, blustering and generally creating a scene. You get what your people need by following your chain of command, presenting your boss with a logical argument in favor of what is required and having the answers to questions you anticipate that the brass hats might pose. Serving as a reasonable and knowledgeable advocate is how you best serve your people in the realm of their safety needs. The same principle holds true for whatever else you need to do to advocate for your officers in their difficult role as peacekeepers.

You have an ethical obligation to defend your people when they do it right. You want your people to do it the right way when it comes to officer safety. That means handcuffing and searching when safety sense says you should, even if the arrestee is 16 years-old and whining up a storm. It means producing and pointing a firearm when you feel your life may be in danger, even if it later turns out the situation was not what it appeared to be. On occasion when your officers do it the right way – the way required by their safety and survival training – they will draw questions and complaints, either from outside or even from within the department. If you want your officers to continue to follow the best practices for safety that you have taught them, you must be prepared at all times to explain and defend their legitimate actions.

As a leader you will have opportunities to speak to the public either in groups or one at a time. Take the opportunity to educate citizens about the difficulty of the law enforcement officer's job, particularly in the area of officer safety. Expect some tough questions and have the courage to answer them honestly. When your agency or your people are under attack simply because safety-conscious cops did their jobs, be prepared to respond to that assault, too. Do it with tact, restraint and diplomacy. Always maintain your professional's demeanor and self-control. But do it all the same.

The same requirement holds true for interagency discussions over what your officers did in the name of safety. Don't throw your credibility away by defending indefensible conduct. But stand up for your people, even to the Big Boss himself, when you know they did the right thing for the right reason. Virtually everyone will respect you for it, win or lose.

You must always look out for your officers' emotional and mental good health. The mental and emotional health of your subordinates must always be of great concern to you. It will do an officer little good to survive the physical threats of a critical incident only to fall prey to the emotional baggage that may accompany it. Surviving on the street today doesn't mean that one won't fall victim to post-traumatic stress disorder and suffer from a total emotional collapse days, weeks, months, or even years later.

The caring supervisor keeps a wary eye on subordinates who have been through potential, life-changing events. A sharp leader knows his people well. He watches for subtle or radical changes in behavior that may suggest professional assistance is needed. And he lets his troubled subordinate know that he will stick with him through whatever trials and tribulations may lie ahead. That kind of loyalty from a leader tends to build much-deserved trust and loyalty in a subordinate.

The wise supervisor realizes that it is not just the life-endangering critical incident that can harm the mental health of a police employee. Peace officers can be laid low by the cumulative stress brought about by a daily diet of bad people and bad situations. Gravely troubled officers who abuse alcohol, drugs and their spouses can be the products of such unabated stress. A few of these officers eventually will hurt others if left to their own ends. More will harm themselves unless successful intervention takes place. You may be able to offer that effective intervention if you remain alert to your peoples' behavior on a day-to-day basis. Meanwhile, you also pay special attention to the officer who has recently gone through a traumatic experience or a series of them, on or off the job. By remaining alert you may be able to save him for law enforcement or even save him, period.

SETTING A GOOD EXAMPLE

You model the right way to do things in all of your actions as a leader. You model the ethics you expect your people to display on and off the job. You show them how to do their work properly in all aspects of the law enforcement officer's task. No one should be surprised that you are at least equally concerned about the mental good health of your officers.

Modeling the on-the-street safety practices you expect of your people is, of course, your first obligation. You do that by employing the "gold standard" for officer safety tactics on every call or contact you make or assist your officers in handling. When you discover that you have made an officer safety mistake, you immediately own up to it and let the officer-witnesses know that you recognize what you should have done instead (tell them!)

Wear your body armor, traffic safety vest and other survival-related equipment, as appropriate. Wear your seat belts anytime that your vehicle is in motion. There is really no valid excuse for doing anything else. Being a role model for safety means doing *everything* the right way, all of the time.

You also want to set a good example in the way you take care of yourself, physically and emotionally. You would look pretty foolish lecturing your people about staying physically fit if you are woefully out of shape yourself. Likewise you would have no moral basis to harangue them about healthy lifestyles if you are a smoker who burns the candle at both ends.

Bad emotional or mental habits are not things that you want to model for your troops, either. If you are prone to fits of anger it will be hard for you to preach about the need to stay in control. If you show little patience or tact in dealing with either the public or your officers you should expect no better from them. And if you want your people to maintain an even keel in the face of adversity you cannot mope or act moody and depressed in front of them. Many of your people want to be like someone they admire: you. The challenge is on you to provide them with something very positive to follow.

Always demonstrate that you consider safety to be Job One for everyone. Your people should understand that there is nothing in the universe more important to you that getting them back home safely at end of watch. You should see and talk safety in just about every police function or operation that involves you. To you, safety should even come ahead of catching the bad guy. You'll always have another try at him tomorrow. You will, that is, if you don't practice and role model poor officer survival today.

Make sure your people see and hear you backing your agency's rules and policies aimed at keeping them alive. If a procedure needs amended to make a given practice safer, do not hesitate to bring it forward on behalf of your employees. They will appreciate your doing so. It might just save someone's bacon.

Remember, also, to be an alert risk manager and safety officer. Point out unsafe practices or conditions and be sure your people know that you expect them to do the same. Safety is everybody's business. There can't be too much of it. Stay careful and stay alive.

Try to stay on the cutting edge of what's new in the way of safety practices, procedures and equipment. Encourage your people to do the same. One or more of you may just pick up on something that has life-saving potential. It may be worth disseminating to the entire organization. Always be willing to talk with your employees about their ideas regarding safety and survival. That's where many of the good ideas come from. But you'll never learn about them if you don't encourage open give and take with your officers, especially where their survival (and yours) is concerned.

SUMMARY

As a leader you will never face a more important task than helping ensure the physical and emotional welfare of your people. As the person they look up to for guidance and direction you will at all times seek to role model the safety and survival conduct you expect of them. You will set the positive example for staying alive that you expect them to follow.

As a safety-conscious leader you will be aware of the most dangerous officer survival errors and how to help defend your employees against them. You will teach officer safety practices and techniques at every learning opportunity. You will identify and correct unsafe behavior whenever you detect it. You will inspect for safe employee practices and you will check up on what your people are actually doing on the street. You will advocate with your bosses for your people's safety and survival equipment needs. You will defend your employees when they are questioned or accused because they did it the right way to stay safe.

As a leader you will strive to be an always-alert risk manager. You will recognize and accept that representing your people and what they reasonably need in the name of officer safety may on occasion put you at least temporarily at odds with your boss. Nonetheless, you will never forget what concerned *you* as a frontline officer (safety, safety, safety!) and you will not cease advocating for your peoples' welfare.

Finally, you will remember that looking out for the welfare of your people requires that you keep your senses attuned to their mental and emotional health, too. Whether they have been involved in a deadly critical incident or are exhibiting the symptoms of accumulated stress, you will act to steer them towards appropriate help if you detect the danger signs of a seriously troubled human being. That is one more way in which you keep your people safe in a too-often dangerous world.

Chapter 11

HOW TO FEED THE NEWSHOUNDS
WITHOUT GETTING BITTEN

Just when the beleaguered law enforcement supervisor thought he had the complex incident scene under control, he sees them coming. "Them," in this case, refers to the ladies and gentlemen of the press. Notepads in hand and camera persons in tow, they are headed straight for him like torpedoes in the water. They smell a story, and they figure that he, the guy with the stripes, can give it to them.

Journalists from the newspaper, television, Internet and radio are drawn to major crime and disaster scenes as ants are lured to a picnic. And they are almost certain to turn for information to the person in charge. Most often, that will be the on-scene supervisor.

Reporters on the scene of a significant police-involved happening is the norm in a nation of information junkies who not only want but demand to know what is going on, and quickly. Unless or until media relations duties are assumed by someone else, such as a departmental Public Information Officer, the first-line supervisor must add press liaison to his or her already lengthy list of duties. Fortunately, the task is one that any capable law enforcement leader can handle with a bit of advance knowledge and preparation. This chapter will provide both.

COPS AND REPORTERS AREN'T THAT DIFFERENT

In the old, unenlightened days cops and reporters tended to fight like conservatives and liberals, which, incidentally, the two groups often were (and are.) For their part, reporters believed that officers of the law were often liars obsessed with secrecy, at least partially because of the need to cover-up their own unlawful or otherwise improper actions. Cops also were frequently seen as clannish, arrogant, and not that bright.

Law enforcers, for their part, tended to see news reporters as Commie, liberal, left-wing sob sisters who contaminated the crime scenes at which they created a circus atmosphere. Journalists likewise were seen as always willing to believe a dirtball over a cop and incompetent to the point of always screwing up an interviewed officer's quote. Reporters, not surprisingly, were further described as clannish liars who were not very bright.

The truth is that a good cop and a good news reporter share a great many common traits. Bosses in both lines of work are seeking ambitious, aggressive, strong-willed people with a good supply of self-confidence. They then train them to part of powerful, highly-visible institutions which see their role as protecting the public from wrongdoers. These employees often display a strong sense of justice and a desire to help the downtrodden, in one way or another. They frequently feel misunderstood, overcriticized and underappreciated by the public. They hang out for mutual support with others very like themselves. And not infrequently they have big egos, cops and journalists alike.

Journalists and peace officers both have important roles to play in today's society. Each has something the other needs in order to do his job more effectively. The reporter needs information. The police often have it. The police need access to the public in order to spread the word about a crime trend or seek public support for a new project or program, or perhaps just to trumpet the good work done by officers. The media can grant them that needed access to the public. Cops and reporters, then, really do need one another. Getting along and cooperating whenever possible simply makes good sense. The law enforcement supervisor can help assure that sort of relationship exists.

Applying his good common sense to his agency's policies and procedures well serves the law enforcement supervisor in the many different aspects of his complex job. The same holds true in the area of police-media relations. Knowing (and following) some time-proven rules and guidelines will aid any police leader in working well with the press while still keeping journalists from despoiling crime scenes and otherwise making officers' work more difficult. It all starts with knowing the rules and how to apply them.

KNOW YOUR MEDIA RULES

Almost every law enforcement organization has a set of policies and procedures governing employees' interaction with representatives of the news media. The supervisor's first step towards assuring that he does a good job of working with the media is assuring that he knows those guidelines inside and out. (It is way too easy to break the rules if one doesn't know what the rules *are*.) Basically, a reporter or photojournalist on a crime or disaster scene has the same rights of movement granted to any other citizen. In other words, if neighbors or passersby are permitted to be in a given area, so is the media rep. One does not lose any rights just because he carries a notepad or camera. But he doesn't grow any extra ones, either.

Whether the rules are written down or not, most police agencies enforce similar, basic media access guidelines. Representatives of the news media cannot be allowed or assisted to break the law. Media reps cannot be permitted to endanger others, including police officers, by their on-scene actions. Members of the media cannot be allowed to destroy evidence or otherwise hinder an ongoing law enforcement operation. From those three, basic rules almost all other police media guidelines sprout.

The truth is that veteran journalists know these rules at least as well as most of the police officers at the scene. They understand the meaning of police barricade tape. They know what they will and won't be allowed to do. That doesn't mean that an overeager photojournalist will not try and push the envelope to get that special, prize-winning picture. It doesn't mean that an aggressive TV reporter won't try to follow officers into a forbidden area.

The police supervisor riding herd on the media reps at an incident scene will need plenty of patience, courtesy and tact in dealing with the press. He knows that losing his temper and promising to put people in jail probably will land him on the evening news, and not in a positive light. He also realizes that cop hands clapped over camera lenses belong to another, now-past era of poor law enforcement-media relations. He understands that taking enforcement action against a recalcitrant reporter should be his absolute last resort for solving a police-media conflict. Before he elects to take such grave action, the supervisor should first consider:

- Did the media misconduct endanger life or property?
- Could the "bad behavior" have been accidental or was it clearly intentional?
- Has the offending journalist done something similar previously?
- Are there witnesses to the misbehavior?
- Was the offender first warned, and if so what was his response?
- Was a scene or investigation compromised by the media misconduct?
- Could the misbehavior have been brought about by unclear or conflicting instructions from law enforcement personnel?
- Does the incident appear to be an isolated one involving an individual or organization known to be normally responsible and ethical?

A lot of supervisory patience displayed on-scene often can prevent a little snafu from blowing up into a major problem in which formal action is required. More often than not, a verbal warning and perhaps a courteous escort out of the forbidden area will be all that is required to solve the crisis. Once more the competent supervisor will have demonstrated his value to the law enforcement organization and the people it must work with in an effective manner.

A final caution is in order: No one has appointed the on-scene supervisor to be chief of the Good Taste Police. On occasion cops' sensibilities will be rightfully offended by the cameraperson intent on getting pictures of a very gory or otherwise upsetting scene, such as a pedestrian fatality involving a mangled child. Officers have no legal standing to prohibit a photojournalist from taking pictures from a public place in which he has a lawful right to be. If his work is in poor taste, it will be up to his boss (or his audience) to chastise him. Deciding which images can and cannot be captured in a public place is not the job of the law enforcement leader.

GIVING A GOOD INTERVIEW

It's a fact that good cops who would not hesitate to chase an armed suspect nonetheless can go jelly-legged when confronted by a young man or woman carrying nothing more lethal that a camera, digital recorder or notepad. To these unfortunates the term "interview" is synonymous with the word "torture." The law enforcement leader cannot afford to be so faint of heart. Fortunately, with just a little advance knowledge of some "tricks of the trade" any leader can represent himself and his employer well while disseminating vital information to the viewing, reading or listening audience.

It is the police leader's goal to be at least as well prepared for the interview encounter as his interviewer is. Telling the truth and nothing but the truth remains his single, best guidepost for engaging in a successful interview. But getting it right begins well before the interview session starts. Some good advice for giving a winning interview includes the following tips.

Figure out who should do the interview. Ideally, the one who has the most facts should do the interview. At the same time, however, an officer who is the most knowledgeable about the details of the crime or incident may be too busy handling the actual situation to have time for a media diversion. As a consequence, the first-line supervisor or other leader may by default become the best person to do the session. Particularly if it is anticipated that the interview may get into matters of policy, it would not be fair to expect the line-level employee to meet the press. The leader is best-suited for the role.

Ask the interviewer what he is seeking and what the questions will be. A professional journalist will not object to being asked what he is going to ask his interview subject. He has a vested interest in producing a good interview product, and he knows that giving his subject a chance to prepare his answers will improve the final results. By having this pre-interview discussion with his interviewer the leader also will be able to tell the reporter if there are areas that he will not be able to answer. A courteous explanation as to *why* should be provided, too. That does not mean, of course, that the questions won't be asked, anyway.

Expect "surprise" questions. The veteran interviewee knows that often he will be asked questions that the interviewer did not mention in advance. This does not necessarily mean that the interviewer is being "sneaky." The interview may simply have gone in an unexpected direction. Or one of the leader's answers may have led the interview off into a new direction. The leader should anticipate some unexpected queries and not overreact to them. If he doesn't know the answer or can't answer, it is perfectly alright to say so. (But it's *never* alright to say "no comment." There are too many better ways of saying essentially the same thing.)

Conduct thorough pre-interview preparations. Before he can give out the facts the leader first has to have them. He can use people, documents, his own observations, or all of these sources to gather the facts to answer the questions he will be asked. He must then double and triple check them for accuracy – disseminating false information is the last thing he wants to do. For that reason, he will never include rumor or unverified "information" in his answers.

Even if he only has time to do it in his head, the wise interviewee will utilize the little time he has available before the interview to rehearse what he plans to say. Doing so will increase his confidence and result in a smoother interview performance. He should realize it is perfectly normal to feel a few pre-interview butterflies. Even some very experienced television newscasters confess to the pre-performance jitters. Some say it helps them stay sharp.

Check your appearance. The law enforcement leader is not vain just because he wants to come across as the professional he is when he appears on-camera. After all, showing up on television with powdered sugar on his dark blue uniform shirt is not the image he wants to leave with his audience. Taking a moment to give oneself a once over in the rearview mirror is a pretty good idea.

Seek a relaxed, but professional image. The leader is seeking to strike a balance here. He does not want to slouch and look slovenly, but neither does he want to come across as a ramrod-stiff, "just the facts" robot. He seeks to communicate confident authority, not egotistical arrogance. Looking the part of a relaxed but in control professional is what the leader is after. His audience needs to know by looking that what he has to say can be trusted, as can he.

Avoid distractions. The audience should be focused on the leader and what he has to say, not on his babbling portable radio, or the chewing gum he is working over. Distracting gestures or body language must be avoided, as well. While the leader likely will have only limited control of the environment at a crime or incident scene, it will be to everyone's advantage that he strives to get far away enough from the action so that his audience can concentrate on what he has to say rather than the sights and sounds in the background. The information he has to impart is too important to get lost in the commotion.

Be quick, be concise, be gone. The typical television news interview is over in 60 seconds or less. The journalist's time constraints will dictate that much of what the interviewee had to say never gets on the air. This is not the time for long and involved explanations or war stories. The supervisor will answer the question he was asked courteously, but in as few words as possible. If the interviewer has time for more details, he likely will ask a follow-up question. Getting to the point right away will help assure that the law enforcement leader gets the most important information placed in front of his newspaper, television, radio or Internet audience.

Maintain eye contact with the interviewer. The idea is for the interviewee to do the same thing he hopefully would do during a conversation with anyone: make eye contact with his conversation partner. This holds true whether the interviewer is on- or off-camera; whether the interview is for the electronic media or the newspaper. Doing so is the courteous thing to do. It also looks a lot more professional (as well as normal) to a home-viewing audience.

Stay calm and in control for the duration of the interview. The viewing, reading or listening audience is looking for indications that the leader is competent, in charge and believable. An interviewee who is sweating, squirming and looking like he very much wants to be somewhere else will not contribute to that positive image. It may take every iota of the acting skill he possesses, but it is mandatory that the police leader looks like the professional he really is. He does that by maintaining his composure and suppressing any visible evidence of discomfort. It's something that good cops do all the time.

If you don't know or can't say, say so. An experienced journalist knows that there are places his law enforcement interviewee will not go in responding to questions. He also realizes that the interviewee probably doesn't know *everything* there is to know about the subject at hand. That doesn't mean he won't ask, all the same. The interviewee's correct response is simply to say so – politely – when he cannot answer a given question. He also should say *why* he cannot answer just now. If the query is one he *could* answer but doesn't have the needed data at the time, he says so and then keeps a promise to get back to the interviewer with the answer as quickly as possible.

Always correct misinformation promptly. Whether it's the interviewer or the interviewee that is responsible for giving out incorrect information, it's up to the interviewee to correct the error right away. That holds true even if a "live" interview is in progress. The same advice holds whether the inaccurate information was given accidentally or otherwise. Presenting an accurate picture of an event or the agency's stand on it is too important to allow an incorrect picture to linger in front of the public. It is in the best interest of both interviewer and interviewed to get it right.

It's alright to ask for a "do over." It's normal for an interviewee to think the session hasn't gone well, when in reality it probably went just fine. (The public does not expect its peacekeepers to be professional speechmakers.) But if it is obvious to the objective leader that he stuttered, stammered and really did do a less-than-acceptable job of being interviewed, unless the interview was broadcast "live" it is perfectly acceptable to request the opportunity to do it over. If the interviewer agrees that a lot of improvement is needed, he likely will grant the interviewee's courteous request. It is in his interest to produce a professional-looking piece, too. If the journalist declines the request, it is entirely possible that the interviewee did a better job than he thought. His wisest course of action is to put it out of his head and move on.

A self-critique will help you get better for the next time. One gets better at doing interviews by doing interviews. It's as simple as that. The smart police supervisor also will ask others whose opinions he respects how he did in his interview performance. It's perfectly fine to ask the interviewer for an on-the-spot critique. Once more, it is likely that the interview subject did better than he thought. Still, an honest self-evaluation can be helpful. Even the most practiced interviewee wants to get better for the next time.

The police interviewee must always guard his earned reputation as a credible professional, even if an interviewer appears biased or the questions unfair. The professional doesn't tell lies, nor does he permit himself to be provoked by an unprofessional or unethical interviewer. The more he looks and sounds like the caring, decent human being that he is, the more he will find that his audience accepts what he has to say as well as his point of view.

There are still more "media interaction" tips to keep in mind. The police leader should avoid the temptation to speak "off the record" with an interviewer unless he knows the individual *extremely* well. Even then, it's risky business, as there is no legal prohibition keeping the reporter from using the irresistible tidbit he was given in confidence. As every veteran cop knows, secrets have a way of not staying secret.

As in the rest of his duties, the law enforcement supervisor can ill afford to play favorites on the job. That holds true for media interviews. Giving an interview to one journalist while deliberately denying another is not playing fair. Only bad feelings will result from the practice. Even though it may be time-consuming, once the leader has agreed to give one reporter access for an interview he is obliged to entertain the journalist's competitors. Fair is fair, after all.

The police leader learned as a rookie to treat all guns as always loaded. He would be wise to likewise regard all media electronic gear as always "on." More than one or two public figures have seen their careers crash in flames following a statement or action made in front of a camera or microphone that they did not realize was "live." The tiny personal communications devices seemingly carried by just about everyone today have further improved the chances for just about anybody to be a *60 Minutes* correspondent. As a consequence, the wise supervisor does or says nothing in public that he would not want broadcast to the whole planet, particularly when he is in the presence of the minions of the media.

By relying on a little skill coupled with an ample supply of common sense the police leader can excel at being interviewed by the news media. Interviewer and interviewee alike can win as each does his job competently and professionally. That's what a good interview is all about.

HOW TO WRITE A NEWS RELEASE

The news release is an important part of the police agency's overall media relations effort. Through it the public can learn what their gun-toting public servants are up to and how they can help their peace-keepers.

Many agencies have a Public Information Officer (PIO) whose duties include producing press releases. But when he is not available or if the agency simply does not have a PIO, the release-writing duties may fall to the law enforcement leader. When that happens the leader needs to know more than *how* to do a release. He also must be able to do one that gets noticed (and used) by the media. A release that doesn't get used is of no use to anyone.

But *when* does the leader and his department do a news release? After all, agencies judged guilty by the media of using news releases for trivial matters often find their future releases ignored altogether. What is considered newsworthy will vary from one locale to the next. Still, several subject areas often merit a release distributed by e-mail, fax or internet posting. Those topics include:

- Major crimes and arrests for them
- Disasters, natural or man-made
- Accidents involving one or more fatalities
- Missing children
- Major organizational or service delivery changes within the agency
- Major new programs, projects or campaigns involving the agency
- Awards recognizing exceptional feats by citizens or police personnel
- Any other action or incident generating or likely to generate a large volume of public or media interest

The supervisor designated to prepare a news release must first determine exactly what it is that his audience wants to know. Most often, his release will need to answer the same questions that should be answered in a good police report: who, what, when, where, why and how. These queries are known to cops and journalists alike as the *Five Ws and an H.* To answer the questions, the release writer must first reach out to the individual who has the needed information, assuming he does not already have it himself. He then must double-check it for accuracy. After the release has been issued is not the time to discover that it contains misspelled names, incorrect addresses or other key errors. (If, in spite of everyone's best efforts, errors are discovered anyway, it is vital that every media agency receiving the release also receives the correction right away.)

The release's most important points should go into the first sentence or two. Journalists call this the *lead* of a news item. The idea is that a busy reader, listener or viewer who only has time to grab the first line or two will nonetheless get the main points of the story. Everything else in the release should be in descending order of importance. And just how lengthy should a news release be? Generally speaking, a release should cover no more than a single, double-spaced page. It should not read like a police report, as the extensive details often found in a good police report have no place in a news release.

The rookie news release writer can learn a lot by reviewing press releases done by his own or other law enforcement agencies. (Some agencies post them on their web sites.) He also can learn from reading and watching news stories done by media professionals. There's nothing wrong with copying success.

There are some other things the police boss can do to spread the word about what his agency and its people are up to. There are also some mistakes that can be avoided by the careful news release writer. Consider, for instance:

DO be sure the release has actual value. News releases that carry little or no news value will wear out the agency's credibility with the media.

DO stick to the facts. The author's opinions, biases or exaggerations have no place in a news release. Neither do rumors.

DO keep the release as brief as feasible without omitting important facts.

DO assure that the name and contact information for the agency and the release's writer are prominently displayed in the release. The telephone numbers and e-mail address of the writer are vital for the reporter trying to obtain clarifications or additional details.

DO put a title or heading on the news release to give the recipients an idea of what it is about. Realize, however, that journalists likely will come up with their own headline or lead-in if they use the release's contents.

DO keep a copy of the release for future reference.

DO use the civilian version of times and dates in the release. There are a lot of people out there, journalists included, who don't know that 1800 means 6 p.m.

DO use the active as opposed to passive voice in the release. That means that "Officer John Smith captured the burglar," not "the burglar was captured by Officer John Smith."

DO keep words, sentences and paragraphs short and concise.

DON'T wait until the last minute to prepare a news release. That may be when everyone is busiest and errors can creep in more easily.

DON'T forget contact information so that the reporter has someplace to go for more details.

DON'T fail to proofread the release multiple times before it goes out. Have a critical colleague proof it, too. A document that speaks for the whole agency should not be rife with mistakes.

DON'T omit any news organization that might be even remotely interested in the news. (Be sure your media contact list is up to date.)

DON'T be disappointed if the release does not get used. Space and time limitations and the quantity and importance of other news could get it pushed aside. Nonuse likely has nothing to do with the writer's skills.

It is also worth remembering that the news release may not satisfy the information hunger of a good reporter, no matter how well it has been written. The writer should anticipate follow-up requests for yet more details. That's one reason why a name and contact information must be provided with the release. Even though he has done an excellent job of crafting a news release, the leader's job may not be quite done yet. However, with a little patience and old-fashioned courtesy lacing his answers he is nearing the finish line of a job well done.

Sometimes there is nothing as useful as an example to understand how it's done. Two sample news releases follow. They demonstrate how some of the journalist's most basic tools can be used to help the law enforcement leader. Properly used, these tools will aid the news release writer in getting his message successfully placed in front of his citizen audience. One release reports on a criminal event; the other relates significant departmental news. Note that each makes use of a good introductory lead and seeks to answer the vital "5 Ws and an H."

Sample 1

N E W S   R E L E A S E

Tumbleweed Police Department
3210 70th Avenue
Tumbleweed, TX 76910

TUMBLEWEED POLICE MAKE ARREST IN HOMICIDE

Tumbleweed Police officers responding on a report of gunshots heard at approximately 11 p.m. Friday night discovered the body of an adult male in the parking lot of the Dewdrop Inn, 1208 Main Street. The man, whose identity has yet to be released by the Smith County Coroner's Office, was pronounced dead on scene by a deputy coroner.

Arrested inside the lounge by TPD officers was Tamera Toots, age 49, of Sweetwater, Texas. She was lodged in Smith County jail pending the filing of First Degree Murder charges.

An investigation continues into the incident. It is not anticipated that additional details will be released prior to Monday morning.

Sgt. Marvin Monroe
Public Information Officer
Tumbleweed Police Department
Telephone (325) 655-0000
e-mail: marvin.monroe@tpd.com

Sample 2

NEWS RELEASE

Tumbleweed Police Department
3210 70th Avenue
Tumbleweed, TX 76910

TUMBLEWEED POLICE ANNOUNCE NEW DEPUTY CHIEF

Tumbleweed Police Chief George Jones today announced the appointment of TPD Captain Melrose Weasel, 49, as the department's new deputy chief. Weasel, an 18-year veteran of the department, replaces Deputy Chief Wally Wacko, who retired last month. The promotion is effective immediately.

Captain Weasel began his career with TPD as a patrolman in 1994. Since then he has served as a Patrol sergeant, detective supervisor and watch commander before being promoted to captain in 2008. He is presently in charge of the department's Patrol Division.

Weasel holds a Bachelor's Degree in Criminal Justice from Texas State University. He has graduated from leadership courses sponsored by the Southern Police Institute and the Police Executive Research Forum.

Captain Weasel and his wife Mary reside in the city. They have two children, Samuel, age 21, and Betty, age 18.

Sgt. Marvin Monroe
Public Information Officer
Tumbleweed Police Department
Telephone (325) 655-0000
e-mail: marvin.monroe@tpd.com

SUMMARY

Spreading the word about crime, crime prevention and the good work done by his people has always been an important job for the law enforcement leader. Today's electronic technology has made his job a bit easier. Only the unwise boss will fail to take advantage of every possible means of letting the taxpaying audience know what his agency is doing to keep them safe.

Working with the minions of the media must be listed among the many responsibilities of today's law enforcement supervisor. While he may not have to do it daily, the well-rounded leader must be *prepared* to take center stage (and look competent doing it) whenever necessary. Depending upon his assignment within the law enforcement agency, one leader will draw more media attention than another. But however often he must face the notepads, cameras and microphones the sharp leader will be ready to show himself and his organization in the best light possible. Who can say – he might even have some fun doing it.

Chapter 12

HOW TO WORK FOR SOMEONE

Just about everybody has a boss or several of them. You may be fortunate enough to work for a virtual saint or you may labor under the lash of someone at the virtual other end of the goodness scale. More likely you work for a very human individual who is positioned somewhere between the absolute poles of Heaven and Hell.

Just as you have expectations of the people who work for you, your boss reasonably expects that you do certain things and refrain from doing others in your role as his or her loyal subordinate. Your boss almost certainly expects that you tell him the truth and keep him well informed about the activities of the work group under your command. He expects that you will not be guilty of disloyalty, in whatever manner he defines that term. And he definitely wants you to keep him out of any trouble that the exercise of your leadership skills might have prevented. There is all of that, and more.

This chapter is aimed at helping you bolster your skills at working for someone while serving your own interests as a leader who wants to advance in the organization in which he is a key member. It will help you grasp what your boss wants from you, and what he does not want to see in his subordinates. It also will help you troubleshoot the "boss challenges" that are inevitable in every superior-subordinate relationship. Most important, it will help you become a better leader.

WHAT YOUR BOSS WANTS

There are a number of things you want from your subordinates. It's a good bet that your own boss expects the same things of you, and then some. Those expectations probably include the following:

To receive from you the unvarnished truth at all times. You likely have said it yourself: your reputation for truth and integrity is your most precious asset as a law enforcement leader. It's true. Your boss will expect that reputation for credibility to be accurate. He will expect you to tell him the truth at all times, even if hearing the truth will make him less than happy. Unless he's stupid, your boss also will expect that you tell him the *whole* truth, unfiltered and unvarnished. You need to have the correct information in order to make good decisions; so does your boss. He expects to get it from you. He also expects that you will not omit relevant parts of the story that he needs to hear. After all, lying by omission is still lying.

Your complete loyalty. If you dislike or distrust your boss so intensely that you can barely stand to work for him, affairs have reached a sad state, indeed. The only way for you to solve the problem may be to move on. But until you have exited the organization you ethically owe your supervisor your complete loyalty. That means you do not undermine his decisions and directions nor speak badly about him in front of your subordinates. You do not participate in organizational plots or intrigues to undo your supervisor, nor do you start or relay gossip about him. You are, in a few words, as loyal to your boss as you would expect your subordinates to be to you.

Your reliable support when things get tough. You have an occasional rough day (or week, or month). Odds are your boss does, too. That is when he would appreciate a supportive word, gesture or hand on the shoulder. Just as you do when things are not going well, your boss probably would like to know that he is not in the struggle all alone. Let your boss know that you've noticed that something is troubling him. Ask him or her what it is you can do to help. Then, assuming that it's ethical and lawful, do it without fanfare. Providing your boss with your sincere support at a difficult time can greatly strengthen the working bond between the two of you. Who knows, he just may offer you the same hand when you really need it one day. Regardless, you will have done the right thing for another human being in need.

Your competent, professional advice and information. You are your leader's technical, professional expert in your line of work. It is entirely possible, even likely, that he does not know nearly as much about your area of expertise as you do. That's alright. One of your obligations to your boss is to advise him accurately regarding the details of the job that he may have never known or simply forgotten. It is important, naturally, that you advise him correctly. If you do not know the answer to something he has asked about, don't guess. Let him know that you'll do some checking and get him the correct information. Then, do it without fail.

To be kept in the know about what's going on beneath him. It would be the unusual boss who knows as much about what's going on and being said in the trenches as you, his subordinate, knows. Don't start or carry rumors and half-truths, but do keep your boss advised on important happenings below him. Never shade the facts to serve your own purposes – or someone else's. Just report accurately on what's happening and allow your leader to form his own conclusions. Providing your boss with accurate information is yet another way in which you demonstrate your absolute honesty to him or her.

Your best work, without exception. You doubtlessly are good at what you do. Allow your supervisor to enjoy the benefits of your considerable abilities. Never get lazy or submit less than your best effort when your boss gives you an assignment or asks you a question. Endeavor to be at the top of your game at all times. Doing a good job always will help you get noticed for advancement yourself, if that thought interests you. Even if it does not, doing your best at all times is something you do for your own pride and professional ethics. It is the right thing to do.

CARDINAL SINS TO AVOID

A successful marriage requires you to refrain from doing certain things. A true friendship requires the same. It should not come as a surprise to you that a trusting and mutually beneficial working relationship with your supervisor requires that you avoid some of these same, critical errors. To have that positive relationship with your boss you must steer clear of these critical, perhaps fatal cardinal sins:

Lying to your boss, even by omission. Tell the truth, the whole truth, and nothing but the truth to your boss at all times. Once he has discovered that you have lied to him it is unlikely that the damage ever can be totally repaired. It may well be a career ender for you, at least insofar as that boss is concerned. There's a way to avoid the whole disaster, of course: don't lie.

Surprising or embarrassing your supervisor. You don't like being surprised by something a subordinate should have told you about. You don't like being embarrassed by something one of your people has done or said. Your own supervisor doesn't like it, either. Do your best to avoid either of those things ever happening because of something you did, or failed to do. You probably won't be perfect here; life itself is imperfect. Just do your best at all times. When in doubt, tell your boss. Like yourself, he likely would rather be over-informed than ill-informed. Work closely with your people

Blaming him for unpopular decisions or directions. This one can mean sudden career death for the subordinate supervisor dumb enough to try it. You don't have much use for those who attempt to lay their own failings or unpopular calls off on others. Chances are your boss does not much care for them, either. You and he would likely agree that those pulling this stunt lack backbone and the courage of their own convictions. They certainly are not qualified to be leaders. Remember never to fall victim to what may *seem* the easier way out at the moment. It isn't. Own your actions and decisions, right or wrong, popular or unpopular. You will earn the respect of others, your boss included, in the process.

Pandering to your employees. It is unlikely that your people are going to get everything they want. Virtually no one ever does. Promising them the moon and then blaming others (like your boss) when the lunar gifts do not appear is a scheme guaranteed to blow up in your face. Do not make promises you know you cannot keep. Don't make unreasonable statements in front of your people. Promising things you cannot deliver will not endear you to anyone, especially your supervisor. Be fair to your people. Represent their legitimate interests. But never pander to gain your subordinates' good will. There's a good chance that you'll only earn their ire when you cannot deliver.

It's worth saying one more time: Do not criticize your boss or his decisions in front of your people, either. That amounts to pandering in the first degree. The penalty for conviction could mean a death sentence for your leadership career.

Showing fear or self-doubt. Like your subordinates, your boss wants to know that no challenge is too great for you to handle. He needs to know that you won't run or come unglued, even if inside you that is exactly what's happening. He needs to know that you are his strong rock in the flood. He needs to know that you are unswervingly sure of yourself and your abilities. He needs to know that you will take care of him. Even if it calls for your best acting skills, never let your boss see you sweat. Let him know that he is much better off with you in charge as opposed to someone else. You will indeed take care of him. No fear. No doubt. No problem.

Upstaging your boss. It's a natural thing to want to look good and be known for your abilities. Doing so builds self-esteem and self-confidence. That's good. Just don't strive to look better than your boss in the organization in which you are both a part. If it happens anyhow, so be it. Just don't work at eclipsing your boss's work and reputation. Share your triumphs, whatever they may be, with him. Praise him on occasion. After all, as your supervisor he doubtlessly put you on the right track to success. Doubtlessly. Or something like that. That goes hand in hand with never criticizing your supervisor publicly. He is your boss and you are proud of him and his abilities. If you aren't, keep quiet about it. Eventually others will see the situation for what it really is.

Participating in organizational intrigue. Don't do it. When the long knives come out lots of people can get hurt, including you. Your ethics as well as your good common sense should tell you to remain above the internal turmoil that most organizations seem to go through at one time or another. Likely your supervisor will want you to stay out of the plotting and power plays, too. He'll want you to spend your time and energies on your assigned duties, not palace coups and character assassinations. Chances are you also will feel better about yourself if you stay out of the game playing.

DOING YOUR BOSS'S JOB

There are a lot of good reasons for spending some time with your boss. Perhaps the best one is simply to get to know him better. You may discover that he's a pretty decent fellow, after all. You also can learn what's important to him, what his hot buttons are and any special areas of worry, expertise or interest he may have.

By engaging your boss in conversation as often as possible you also can determine to at least some extent how much he knows – or doesn't know – about the operations for which you are responsible. Knowing that will tell you how much subtle "educating" you will need to do with him concerning your own duties. Gently correct any misperceptions he may harbor. He will be a stronger advocate for you and your people if he understands what you all are doing and why. It would be a mistake to assume that he understands everything just because he's the boss.

Do not believe that old line about never volunteering for anything. Following that poor advice will not serve you well in your leadership career. Volunteering for additional assignments will do more than leave a favorable impression with your supervisor, as important as that is. Taking on extra work, especially the kind that your boss otherwise would do himself, will boost your leadership education and experience levels within the organization. Learning what your boss does and how he does it will assist you greatly in taking over his job one day, if that is your plan. By stretching your knowledge base you aid the organization at the same time you help yourself. Everybody wins, including your boss.

Virtually everyone has some special abilities, skills and strengths. You do, too. Whether yours are technical in nature or are more in the area of "people skills," you owe your leader and your agency the best of what you have. Share your special talents for the good of everyone involved, yourself included. Making your supervisor's life a little better can benefit you, too.

If you are a good writer and you know that your boss struggles in that area or just plain doesn't like to write, offer to help him with those lengthy memorandums or other writing assignments. If math is your strong suit but you know from talking with boss that he truly hates doing those financials, offer to give him a hand. (Double- and triple-check, by the way, to be sure you've done an assignment for your boss correctly!) You likely will do much more than gain your boss's gratitude. You additionally will pick up valuable experience that will help you advance your leadership career.

Make it clear to your supervisor that you *want* to learn his job. Let him know that you want to advance your career and spend a long time with the organization. Ask him to share his knowledge in coaching and mentoring you. Most good bosses welcome the opportunity to help prepare the next generation of leaders. (You do, right?) Promise to be a good and attentive learner. You might just be surprised at your boss's response. Like you, he or she may be quick to see that both of you can win.

SOLVING BOSS PROBLEMS

It has been said that if you and your boss are having difficulties, only one of you really has a problem. And it isn't your boss. That is one of the realities of working for somebody. As a consequence it will be greatly to your benefit to assure that friction with your supervisor is kept to an absolute minimum and salved as quickly and painlessly as possible when it does occur, as inevitably it will.

You are truly fortunate if you can honestly state that you have never had a bad boss. Unfortunately, there are more than a few of them out there. Bad bosses come in various forms ranging from the mildly irritating to the outright criminal. Their bad behavior can manifest itself in everything from sexual harassment to racial discrimination, employee favoritism, and bullying.

Bad bosses generally do not solicit evaluations of their performance from their subordinates. They don't much care for criticism of any kind, except the kind that they direct in great quantity at others. Many of them are very unpleasant to be around.

There is no easy way of telling the Boss from Hell that's what he is. The good news is that even difficult bosses are generally not so far out on the scale of nastiness that you cannot work with them at all. You can do some things to assure your organizational as well as mental survival. Some careful work melded with reasonable caution on your part often can make a less-than-ideal relationship at least a tolerable one.

Some leaders seek to lessen the stress brought on by dealing with a difficult boss by minimizing their contact with the offender. That can help and should not be overlooked as a partial solution. But while it may feel like it is working in the short term it really won't solve a bad boss problem over the long haul.

The decision to confront your boss with a relationship problem of his making is a call that only you can make. If your experience with him has taught you that doing so only will result in a detonation and fallout that comes down on your head, that may not be a smart option. But other leaders like you have found that openness and candor can have good results. Your personal knowledge of your supervisor and his or her personal foibles will have to serve as your best guidance on how to proceed.

Talking honestly and openly with your boss does not have to begin with complaints and accusations. You can ease into the conversation by telling your boss (in a private setting, of course) how his behavior – whatever it is – makes you feel. Believe it or not, some bad bosses actually do not realize that they are bad bosses. By addressing your concern to your supervisor in a quiet, nonconfrontational manner you may be able to get your message across without triggering a boss explosion.

A message to your boss might go something like this: "Boss, I know you would never intentionally hurt me. You're too good a person for that. But when you call me down in front of the other guys it really embarrasses me and makes me feel pretty worthless. I always want to avoid disappointing you and I want to give you my best, but if you could tell me these things privately I'd surely appreciate it."

With this approach the boss is given a face-saving way out if he wants to take it. He didn't know he was doing wrong. It was accidental. You obviously still want to please him. He can show what a good guy he is by working through this with you. Or something like that.

It won't work every time. But it won't fail every time, either. It's worth a try for the value it may produce. If it does not result in any changes in your boss's behavior you probably have not lost anything by trying. It was worth the effort. Also, keep in mind that your boss may take your message to heart and attempt to implement some changes in his actions *even if he denies the behavior you told him about.* His ego may keep him from acknowledging the accuracy of your grievance.

A bad boss problem unaddressed is unlikely to improve on its own. Like a serious illness, it requires treatment to get better. Sulking or gossiping about it to your peers won't help and may actually worsen your discomfort. If the gossip you started gets back to your problematic supervisor you have only succeeded in magnifying your problems.

You and you alone have to make the decision of how far to go in confronting your bad boss problem. Talking to your boss's boss should be viewed as the response of last resort, but it may be appropriate depending upon the seriousness of the situation you are facing. Criminal conduct or sexual harassment by your boss are obvious offenses mandating that you go over your boss's head in seeking redress. There are other serious violations requiring the same approach. As uncomfortable as it may make you to go this route, your personal integrity, welfare and the welfare of the organization and its members will require you to act.

Directly confronting a bad boss problem in an honest and tactful manner is oftentimes the best way of addressing it. If you encounter stiff resistance from your first attempt, you may have to try again later. But by tactfully providing your supervisor with an opportunity to save face ("I had no idea!") you may be able to secure the needed change in behavior, or at the very least mitigate his difficult conduct. Trying is worth your earnest efforts. Too much is at stake to permit the actions of a bad boss to reduce the effectiveness of a good law enforcement leader: you.

SUMMARY

There are many reasons why leaders fail to realize their full potential, but up near the head of the pack has to be the failure to connect effectively with their own supervisor. Understanding what your boss wants and expects is important to your success as a leader in your organization. Equally vital is the need for you to build a relationship of mutual trust with your supervisor. Neither of you will be satisfied with the relationship if that bond does not exist. Excellent communication between the two of you will have to exist if that kind of relationship is to happen.

There are cardinal rules to remember in working well with your supervisor. Telling him the truth at all times is but one of them. Likewise, there are things to be avoided at all costs if you are to maintain a positive working connection with your supervisor. Among the greatest sins are allowing your boss to be surprised or embarrassed and trying to make yourself look better to your subordinates by making your supervisor out to be the bad guy.

Let your boss know that you will look out for him or her. Be prepared to educate him about what you and your people are doing and why. Share your credits and accolades with him. Avoid engaging in organizational politics at your boss's expense. Never show fear or uncertainty in your boss's presence – he needs to be able to rely on you as a rock in tough times. Realize that, in the end, you may have to change (without changing your ethics) to work with your boss's style, as he is unlikely to change to suit you. But never surrender your principles in the process.

It is highly likely that in order to succeed as a leader you will have to command the support of your own boss. Work honestly, ethically, and diligently to earn it.

Chapter 13

HOW TO SURVIVE YOUR ORGANIZATION

Law enforcement leaders have perished doing the jobs they loved, and not always in a car wreck or from an offender's bullets. Heart attacks, strokes and suicides have claimed their tragic toll, too. In more than a few instances the cause of their death has been the accumulating stress from years spent doing a very difficult job. In yet other cases police leaders have not died in harness but have seen their careers ended too soon by health problems brought on by the stresses of the job. Others still have been terminated from employment due to engaging in behavior brought about by stress and the poor choices made in reacting to it.

It does little good to survive the perils of the street only to fall victim to the dangers of organizational life. There is street survival and there is organizational survival. As a leader you must master them both if you are to stay both physically and emotionally healthy throughout a long, productive and rewarding law enforcement career. You still must be prepared to face the threats that the street brings. But you must be at least as well prepared to handle and deflect the challenges brought from the almost inevitable organizational turmoil, politics, and intrigues of the police agency and the larger governmental entity of which it is a part.

Just as your body armor helps to protect you on the street, the attitude, lifestyle and demeanor you project will help shield you *off* the street, too. It should aid you in maintaining a healthy attitude about your important job while avoiding some of the pitfalls that have cut short some of the effective careers of other law enforcement leaders.

This chapter provides sound, common sense advice for surviving the organization you are proud to serve. It's the very same organization that on rare occasions does not seem equally proud of you. At least that's how it probably feels. The advice includes some hints for developing and maintaining a positive attitude about what you are doing.

YOUR ATTITUDE IS SHOWING

The best way to get through any tough challenge is to maintain a good attitude. You have heard that since elementary school, and it's still true. It is not always easy maintaining a positive outlook in the face of crisis and adversity. But doing so will help you get through the tough spots. Here are a few suggestions for getting it done.

Smiling won't break your face. No one is saying you should go through life eternally showing off the 72 pearly whites of a television pitchman. A forced smile isn't sincere and the people you meet will know it. There are times, of course, when smiling is not appropriate anyhow, such as when the information you have to pass along is bad if not tragic. Smiling at a time like that would make you look worse than idiotic. But nobody likes a sourpuss who goes through life glowering, either.

Many people will avoid, if possible, the individual who appears forever about to commit suicide – or bite somebody's head off. What most of those same people are looking for is sincerity and a generally pleasant demeanor. That is the attitude and demeanor you should strive for in your interactions with others. If you are the kind of human being you should be as a leader, that will leave you with a pleasant expression most of the time. Who knows, it could even lead to a real smile in the very next moment.

Gravitate towards positive people. Sad people will make you sad. Too much time spent around bitter, always-negative people will make you bitter. Granted, life dictates that you cannot be around happy, bubbly people all of the time. But you do have it within your power to avoid people you know to be negative as much as you possibly can.

One sergeant recalled an experience from early in his leadership career. "I would come to work at night happy, energetic and ready to go lead my people in putting crooks in jail. Then I'd spend 30 minutes drinking coffee with Sergeant X and I'd be practically suicidal. Nothing was ever good or right, at least according to him. I soon learned to ration the time I spent around him and I was a much happier person."

Practically every organization has its sour, burned-out Sad Sacks. Spend as little time in their company as possible. Instead, endeavor to hang out with the positive people in your organization. By simple observation it won't take you too long to figure out who they are. They will be good for you. Some of your own good vibes just might rub off on them, too.

Be self-confident but curb your ego. There is often only a hair-thin line separating self-confidence from arrogance. You want to have plenty of the former, but avoid the latter like a rabid pit bull. If they are going to follow you, your people will need to be confident in your abilities. Part of that confidence they will build from seeing how you react in moments of stress when real leadership is needed. They will want to see that you are competent and have solid faith in your own competency. But false bravado and fake courage they don't want to see. Detecting either will make them doubt your true abilities.

Try hard to separate your ego from your job and your relationships with your subordinates and superiors. Try to remain modest at the same time and you will know that you can master just about any challenge that comes your way. Cops have a knack for keeping their bosses humble. Be sure that they don't see a need to cut you down to size.

Admit it when you're wrong. The first step towards fixing a mistake is admitting that you made it in the first place. Doing so will not diminish you in the eyes of your boss and your subordinates. Rather, admitting that you can err likely will increase your credibility with them. Like them, you are human. Humans make mistakes from time to time.

There's one more thing you need to do when you realize that you have made a mistake. Do your very best to repair any damage that may have resulted. That includes apologizing to anyone affected by your error. Once again, doing so does not show weakness. It shows that you are a "normal" and decent person who can be both liked and trusted.

You don't have to win *every* time. You probably have known someone who was so competitive and/or ego-driven that he had to win every contest, come out on top in any debate or argument and just generally show himself as superior to everyone else. There's a good chance that you were not overly fond of this individual. Odds are that the people you work with feel the same way about this kind of character. They neither like nor admire him.

Realize that you do not have to diminish others in order to elevate yourself. Just as you can make and admit the occasional mistake, you also can afford to lose an argument or some other contest. By showing yourself to be human you will increase the stock others put in you. And that's something you will want to have as a leader.

Remember the Golden Rule. What you learned as a kid in kindergarten still has value for you as a leader. It isn't complicated, but it will work wonders. Treat others as you would have them treat you. If you want your boss to regard you with respect and honor your views and opinions, you must regard your own subordinates in a like manner. It worked for you as a youngster; it will still work now that you are a leader. The Golden Rule truly is golden for the benefits it can bring to your relationships with others.

Realize that there will be frustrations and disappointments. You should have established a career track for yourself by now. You should follow it to the best of your ability. At the same time you must realize that the best plans get sidetracked sometimes. That's life. Things happen. And that doesn't mean you will be denied your career goals. Your arrival at the end point where you are seeking to go simply may be delayed for a bit. Life doesn't have a copy of the script you wrote for yourself.

One talented sergeant who had scripted out a personal career plan for advancing through the organization found his plans delayed by an untimely disciplinary suspension. He persevered and recovered his career momentum only to have his plans derailed again by serious illness at home. He got past that barricade, too, and resumed his forward progress. He eventually reached the career goals he was seeking. He simply got there a little later than he had planned. He arrived with a bit more experience and worldly knowledge aboard. As a consequence, he was almost certainly a better leader. You can do the same. Persevere in the face of adversity. Odds are you will get where you want to go.

Know that many bad things have a shelf life. Most of the negative events that feel like a Big Deal on Monday will be forgotten or at least greatly diminished in negative impact by Friday. That's simply how the human mind works, and it's good news if you happen to be the one responsible for the bad news on Monday. There are exceptions, of course. If you, for instance, decide to solve your boss problems by shooting him, that particular act probably isn't going to be forgotten or forgiven anytime soon. But murder and mayhem provide an exception to the rule. Right after you have committed a particularly egregious or embarrassing error it certainly may seem like you will never be let up off the floor. The good news is that you will. Life will go on and so will you. It's going to be alright. Realize that and get back to the vital business of leading.

PITFALLS TO AVOID

As you go about handling your leadership tasks you will encounter all kinds of people and situations. Some of each will be good and some of each will be not so good. As an intelligent observer you will be able to learn a lot from both kinds. One thing that life and experience will continue to teach you is that it is better to avoid falling into a bad situation than taking the plunge into one. Your own experiences plus the unfortunate failings of others should help you identify many of the dangers. Sound advice for avoiding these hazards includes the following:

Don't hang out with poisonous people. Like the negative folks, venomous ones will bring you down, too. These are the individuals and cliques that appear to be continually plotting to "get" somebody, whether it's the chief or their watch commander. Oftentimes they are willing to connive, lie, and commit other unethical acts as they scheme to carry out their plot. Not infrequently the members of these cabals get so immersed in their plotting that they can focus on little else (like work, for instance) and end up getting fired. Or they may slither along for years, sowing hatred and discontent wherever they go. Being a part of such a group likely will be a career-ender for the leader foolish enough to jump on their downhill-to-Hell wagon. Stay clear and survive.

Don't be where common sense says you shouldn't be. Like at a party that's getting out of control, for instance, or off-duty in a bar that you know is full of cop-hating characters, or maybe out on the town with a snootful of liquor and a partying companion that you *know* you should not be with. You talk to your troops about listening to the little officer safety voice that tells you to stop what you're doing and do something else. You must be attentive to the same little voice that is telling you, however quietly, that being where you are and doing what you are doing is likely to have very bad career consequences for you.

Your next course of action should be to cease, desist, and depart.

Don't allow your job to become all-consuming. You need some time away from the job and its worries and challenges in order to maintain your mental and emotional health. It's really no more complicated than that. Becoming a full-fledged workaholic truly could kill you. It's happened to law enforcement leaders before and almost certainly will again. You are more than your job. You may be a parent, spouse, lover and friend, to name only a few of your possible, additional roles.

There are more important things to be consumed by than work, as important as that is to a good leader like you. Living a good and fulfilling life off the job is one of them. That you owe to yourself and those who care about you.

To stay healthy, you must strive to avoid allowing your job, as important as it is, to define you. Being a leader means taking control. That includes taking control from a job that would define *you* if given the opportunity. Take charge and stay alive.

Don't participate in organizational plots, schemes and power plays. This piece of sound advice is closely related to the equally-solid recommendation that you stay away from poisonous people. In too many twenty-first century organizations it seems that somebody or a group of somebodies are always scheming to get one-up on somebody else. In the process a lot of time and energy get wasted and bad feelings and recriminations are often the end result. Alliances are formed and broken. Quite often, the losers in these power plays end up unemployed or otherwise penalized. Unfortunately, law enforcement agencies are not immune to these destructive games. Indeed, there are jurisdictions where it seems that at least as much effort is put into this destructive behavior as goes into serving the public's safety. Steer clear of this game playing and protect your career. It also happens to be the right and ethical thing to do.

Don't cheat your employer. Your boss and your employer have certain, reasonable expectations of you. Like, for instance, that they will get your best effort at all times and that you'll turn in (at least) 40 hours of work for 40 hours of pay. It is also fair for your supervisor to expect that you will protect his confidences and otherwise show loyalty to him so long as he performs his own job honestly and ethically.

Cheating is always wrong, whether you are cheating the taxman or betraying your employer through shoddy work and unethical practices. Don't bend the rules and do not associate with those who do. Take appropriate action when you determine that someone else is breaking the rules. (Bad behavior flourishes when no one has the guts to do anything about it.) Cheating is not something that a law enforcement leader does.

Don't be a jerk. Treat others in the manner in which you would have them treat you. You don't have to scream at and belittle your subordinates to prove that you are the boss. (They already know that.) Neither do you need to discipline more harshly than the infraction requires or embarrass your employees to punish poor performance. In other words, be the kind of person you would like to see in the others with whom you must interact each workday. When it comes to friendships, be the kind of friend you would like to have, on and off the job. Be nice. It's really not that complicated.

HOW TO GET FIRED

There are at least as many ways to self-destruct as there are means for succeeding in any organization. That rule of thumb applies to the agency you are a part of. Probably the most complete form of self-destruction comes with the proverbial pink slip. As a supervisor you have seen subordinates get the boot as a result of not-so-smart behavior. Doubtlessly you have witnessed a few of your peers and superiors go down in flames, too. Clearly you want to avoid the behavior that brought on the untimely end of these unfortunates. If you earnestly want to do that, here are some career-ending behaviors you'll want to avoid at all costs. Pull any of these tricks and you have greatly increased your chances of getting fired:

Lie to your boss. As you know, integrity and honesty are the hallmarks of a leader. Liars have neither. Lying to your supervisor is probably the supreme example of showing him or her absolute disrespect. Once the falsehood is found out it will be all but impossible to restore the level of faith and trust that your supervisor previously placed in you. With that bond gone, it is difficult to see how the relationship can survive.

Repeatedly embarrass or disappoint your boss or your department. There are many ways to bring embarrassment to your supervisor and your employer. Committing illegal, unethical or immoral acts probably leads the pack of cardinal sins. Repeatedly falling short in the work you have promised to do trails close behind as a career-ender. Everybody makes mistakes and any reasonable leader permits his underlings their fair share. But if you push your accumulated number of foul-ups beyond that "fair" number, whatever it is, you should expect dire consequences.

Break the law or the rules. You do not like to have chronic rule-breakers among your subordinates. Your boss (and her boss) probably don't much like it, either. The consequences can be even worse if the rule-breaking includes an actual violation of a statute. Do that and you may find yourself in legal trouble as well as unemployed. Law enforcement organizations cannot afford to employ people who break the law, especially when the alleged lawbreaker holds supervisory rank.

Be involved in a high-profile scandal. You may have heard your boss say it: "I don't want to see your name in the news unless you caught the crook of the century or found the cure for cancer." He may be pulling your leg just a little, but the main thrust of his comment is just what he means. Law enforcement is a calling that demands its practitioners do the right thing always, especially if they see themselves as leaders. In most police agencies today a leader who becomes involved in a well-publicized on- or off-duty embarrassment ranging from a sexual indiscretion to a drunk driving arrest can kiss his career and likely his job good-bye.

Engage in sexual harassment or racial discrimination in the workplace. Law enforcement agencies across the nation have labored long and hard to earn a reputation for treating all employees and customers fairly, equally, and with respect. They are justly proud of having earned this status following years of sometimes-justified criticism for failing to do the right thing. Do anything that tears down today's earned reputation for equality in a harassment-free environment and you should expect to feel the full weight of your organization's disciplinary machinery.

Be guilty of insubordination. Your supervisor expects you to do as you are told as long as you are not being tasked with doing something illegal or unethical. It's nothing different from what you expect of your own employees. You as well as they are welcome to provide divergent points of view, but in the end everyone is expected to obey the lawful directions they have been issued. You may have had a very good reason for changing the instructions you were given. If so, you will be expected to state and explain them. All may yet be well, but if you were deliberately insubordinate to your supervisor without good cause expect to pay a stiff penalty. It's likely the same thing you would do if one of your own subordinates acted in a like manner.

Consistently do stupid things. This big mistake might be said to be the umbrella under which all other errors gather. Here the perpetrator may have disregarded his education, training, life experience and just plain common sense in selecting a course of action (or inaction) contrary to what just about any intelligent individual would follow. Oftentimes stupid behavior originates with mental laziness. Other times it appears to spring forth out of arrogance or a mistaken sense of entitlement. Yet, in other instances it is hard to find any explanation at all. Leadership does not permit mentally lazy behavior. Such behavior would appear to be a big part of stupidity.

LIVING HAPPILY EVER AFTER (IT'S ALL ABOUT BALANCE)

Surviving your own organization is one thing. Having healthy fun while doing it is another. Life is simply too brief to spend in an unhappy or troubled state of mind. There are a number of things that can help you avoid a depressed mind-set and keep your life on the positive side of the ledger, at least most of the time. For some people it's a strong sense of faith. For others it's a personal set of ethics, morals and rules to live by. For yet others the guideposts to a happy life are internalized and largely invisible to the rest of the world. And for others still it is a combination of the preceding with yet more factors thrown in.

Whatever works for you is fine. At the same time, successful leaders have amassed some time-tested advice that may help you to stay on the right side of the road of life while maintaining a successful and contributing law enforcement leadership career. Those proven pearls of wisdom include the following:

Put your family first. Not a few marriages and friendships have ended because someone invested more time and energy in the workplace than in the more important relationships of life. Only you can decide on how you want to meet this challenge. But for most normal human beings the rewards of family and friends trump the values of succeeding on the job. Your goal should be to seek a balance where you can realize the pleasures of both without neglecting those who are your ultimate source of love and support.

Have friends away from the job. There are good people, smart people, nice people in the world who don't happen to be cops. Some of them live near you. Many of them you encounter frequently. A lot of them you genuinely like. Take the risk of considering them your friends. They likely will expose you to some views of life that your law enforcement friends may not have. This diversity of thought and opinion may be good for you. It *will* be good for you to have something to think and talk about besides crooks and police work. Take the risk of expanding your horizons when it comes to friends. It will be mentally healthy for you. You may surprise yourself with just how much you enjoy these pleasant associations.

Have people to talk to. It's the same good advice you give your rookie officers: have someone noncritical to talk with about what troubles, amazes, and concerns you. It applies to you just as much as it does these law enforcement neophytes. Keeping your deepest concerns bottled up inside you will only bring you harm. Have someone – preferably several someones – to talk with openly about what is on your mind. You will be much healthier for it.

Save some time for yourself. Save time away from the job to do what feels good to you. You will need that separation of work and play to maintain your mental equilibrium as well as your physical good health. It matters little what your hobby or interest is as long as it is not self-destructive. (Drinking yourself to oblivion thereby would not qualify as a healthy diversion.) As a leader you scrupulously assign time to other people and projects. Do the same for yourself. Just be sure it's not yet more work.

Stay fit physically and emotionally. Leaders take care of their people. But you cannot care for anyone if you don't take care of yourself first. After all, you can't help your folks if you're not there. Take pains to assure that you *are* there tomorrow and for a long time to come. Look out for yourself. Exercise regularly, eat healthy and avoid self-destructive habits, like smoking or drinking to excess. Get a physical exam on a regular basis. Watch your weight. Never neglect your mental health, either.

Seek to respond to the stresses of your job in a healthy manner. Realize that you, too, have emotions. Don't try to deny them, but seek to understand them, instead. Cops feel and get angry and cry, too. So do leaders. Recognize that it is absolutely alright to be human. Your loved ones and your co-workers likely will appreciate your recognizing that reality.

Keep a positive perspective. Law enforcement certainly exposes its practitioners to sadness and tragedy. You've known that for a long time. The key to your emotional survival revolves around recognizing that fact without allowing bad things to dominate your thinking. There are, after all, a lot of good things in life, too. Things like family, friends, and the professional work done by your subordinates. There is much to be proud of and happy about. Promise yourself to focus on the good rather than the bad. You'll be happier for it and so will those around you.

Never stop reading and learning. There is evidence than an active mind stays alert and healthy much longer than a bored one. That's yet another reason for studying your job and endeavoring always to get better at it. Keeping up to date with law enforcement's professional publications can help you. So can the Internet sites that feature law enforcement and criminal justice news. Just staying up with current events can help, too. In today's world what's going on in the profession can change radically in a very short time. To do your job well and serve the people who depend on you to the best of your ability you cannot afford to depend solely on what you learned in the leadership training of five years ago. Life changes course too quickly for that.

Resolve to keep learning throughout your life. What you learn will help you master the new challenges you will face. That newfound knowledge will help you devise the new solutions you will need for the new problems that no one has even thought of yet.

Have a plan for "afterwards." Start planning today for life beyond the badge. Statistics will show that those who have not planned at all for life after the retirement ceremony often do not handle their newly-idle time well. There's even some indication that they don't live as long as those who have a plan and put it into effect. Modern medicine has extended the time in which today's retirees can expect to live relatively healthy and very useful lives. Whether you want to teach, travel, or do very little for a while, start making *some* kind of plan for what you'll do when you don't have to go to work anymore. That knowledge will make you more comfortable today as well as when the time to implement your plans approaches.

SUMMARY

You cannot take care of your job unless you first take care of yourself. Taking care of yourself means eating healthy, exercising regularly and ditching any life habits – like smoking or drinking to excess – that can hasten your "ultimate termination" date. You also must pay attention to your work-play balance and assure that family and loved ones come before the job. Remain mindful that at the end no sane individual ever said that he wished he had spent more time at work.

Surviving at work means controlling your own ego at the same time you make allowances for the mega-egos of others. It means steering clear of the on- and off-duty pitfalls that have claimed others' leadership careers. The tiger traps that you will need to avoid include starting or passing gossip, participating in organizational plots and intrigue and otherwise demonstrating disloyalty or insubordination to your boss.

You are going to make a mistake from time to time. When you do, admit it and do your best to repair the damage. Learn from your missteps and determine never to repeat them. It is OK to ask for (and grant) forgiveness, as appropriate.

Living happily ever after requires that you maintain a positive, upbeat attitude towards your job and life itself. It requires that you have somebody or – even better – several somebodies that you can talk with openly about whatever is bothering you. Attend to your personal ethics and morals just as earnestly as you manage your physical and emotional health. Maintain solid friendships and never stop learning. Listen to that inner voice that instructs you to be a good friend yourself and never cease helping others.

Doing all of these things will do much more than help you survive your organization. Doing them will help assure that you remain in charge of your life, a life that encompasses a lot more than police work.

Chapter 14

HOW TO PUT IT ALL TOGETHER

There is an awful lot of "stuff" involved in becoming an effective leader. There are a lot of skills to be mastered and more than a few personality traits to be honed and polished. Nobody said it would be easy, but they may have neglected to tell you just how hard it would be, also.

In spite of all that you are getting it done. You *are* an effective leader. Your focus now must be on becoming an even *more* effective one. You already know it can be done because you are doing it. You are getting better and better as your level of education, training, and experience grows.

Putting it all together in order to be the most effective leader you can be calls for you to learn from the painful mistakes made by others. It requires that you establish a reputation with your peers, subordinates, and superiors as someone who can be believed and trusted without exception. Your reputation, you know well, is everything in your line of work. Finally, putting it all together involves helping prepare the next generation of leaders who will guide the organization when you are enjoying a well-deserved retirement. Succession planning is a job for a good leader, too.

This chapter will assist you in putting all of the pieces together. It will help you assemble the "complete package" that a leader must be. This is how it is done.

LEARNING FROM OTHERS' MISTAKES

Over a lifetime you doubtlessly have learned a lot from the mistakes you have made. Everyone does. Some of life's lessons have been disappointing, even painful ones. But you have learned from and remembered them, all the same.

Life has by now taught you than you often can learn as much from the experiences of others as you can from your own. The especially good news is that you often can gather that knowledge without going through the pain that the other person experienced, figuratively or literally. You can learn a lot from the errors of other people.

One veteran police chief put it this way: "Throughout my career I have watched the actions of those above me. In doing that I observed plenty of good things I wanted to emulate if I advanced to their level one day. But I think I learned even more from observing the bad habits and screw-ups of others. Every time I witnessed one of those disasters I made a mental note to never, never do that if ever I was in a position of leadership. I have tried to live by that code and any success I have had has been based on it."

The chief has a point. It is one that you will find useful in determining the kind of leader you are and will be as you advance through the ranks of your organization.

In today's world there is no shortage of images of leaders behaving badly to provide you with examples of things you *don't* want to do as a leader. They range from the local elected official tagged for engaging in sexual harassment of his subordinates to the police chief fired and filed on for outright criminal behavior. These major league gaffes include the national-level politician caught lying to the news media and the nationally-renowned journalist "busted" for inventing the details of her tear-jerking feature story. Indeed, there's plenty of fodder out there for the intelligent leader looking for examples of what *not* to do.

Unfortunately, your colleagues in the field of law enforcement leadership have not been idle when it comes to providing you with negative examples of how to behave as a leader. One case can be found in the police executive who managed to involve himself in a late-night scrimmage with a female barfly at a watering hole in his jurisdiction. Another stands out in the case of the chief who apparently felt he needed to supplement his salary by stealing fuel for his personal car at the municipal gas pumps. And not to be forgotten is the galaxy of police managers and supervisors in a Southern U.S. police department who brought national (and negative) attention to their agency by engaging in sexual misconduct on a wholesale level.

But misconduct by law enforcement leaders does not have to make the headlines for you to learn from it and their always-negative consequences. Tragically, big mistakes by law enforcement officials take place on an almost daily basis across the nation. Most of them don't make the evening news, but all of them hurt people in the agencies employing these misdirected bosses.

You certainly can reinforce what kind of leader you want to be by observing the foibles of others. More than one or two of your colleagues have lost their moral authority to lead through their off-duty behavior. By noting where they have gone wrong you can promise yourself that you will never make a similar mistake. (Naturally, you will then be obliged to keep your promise.)

Off-duty (not to mention on-duty) sexual misadventures have claimed the careers of some of your peers. Once more, noting how these ill-advised personal decisions have cost your colleagues their respect (and perhaps their job) should help you avoid committing similar errors yourself. One of John Wayne's grizzled screen characters may have said it best: "Life is hard; it's harder if you're stupid." Pay attention to the just-plain-stupid acts of others. Avoid the anguish that they bring to their perpetrators. It will make life a little *less* hard for you.

Remember that your badge-toting colleagues are not the only ones who can teach you something about what *not* to do to win friends and influence people as an effective leader. Simply staying up on current events can educate you regarding the mistakes being made by elected and appointed officials as well as private-sector Big Shots around the country – and the world. You can learn what not to do by observing what these unfortunates have done elsewhere. Likewise, you can rely on the mistakes made by your own, larger organization's employees outside of the police department for some lessons on what to avoid doing. Dumb acts committed by a boss in the water department or a leader in finance can prove very useful in adding to your mental list of things NOT to do if you desire to be a successful (and employed) leader.

The list of potentially fatal leadership errors that you might see committed by others for your educational benefit is practically endless but may include:

- Sexual misconduct
- Criminal acts
- Drunk or drugged driving, on- or off-duty
- Patently immoral or unethical conduct
- Acts of gender or racial discrimination
- Serious violations of your employer's rules, policies and regulations
- Insubordination
- Grossly inappropriate use of electronic communications, including texting and the social media.

Learn from the positive actions of others. There are lots of good role models out there. But there are lots of bad ones, too. You can learn a lot from both. In the process you will construct the kind of leader you want to be. Because you paid close attention to the mistakes of others there can be little doubt that the leader you assemble will be a powerful force for good.

YOUR REPUTATION IS EVERYTHING

Before you were a formal leader in your organization you depended on your reputation for integrity and fair play to bolster your reputation as a competent and honorable law enforcement officer. You probably said it yourself: "If you don't have a reputation for integrity, you don't have anything in this business." And you would have been correct.

Your reputation is equally important to your success as a recognized law enforcement leader. While you still must retain your reputation for honesty and integrity as a cop, now added to that requirement is the need to maintain a positive reputation as a leader of law enforcement personnel. You maintain that good reputation through what you do on a day-to-day basis.

You establish your good reputation with your superiors and subordinates primarily through your own actions. Most often these acts have developed in response to the challenges thrown at you by the daily questions and other problems of your job as a leader. The challenge of today may be how you elect to handle a disciplinary situation involving a long-term police employee. Yesterday's challenge may have centered around a complaint on one of your people by a local elected official. Tomorrow's challenge could be something similar or a brand new issue never faced by anyone on your department before. Whatever the case, your people and your bosses will be observing to see how you answer the bell. Will you meet the challenge head-on or attempt to deflect it elsewhere? Will you show both intelligence and courage in the solution you develop? Will you be both decisive and fair? On all of these things your reputation as a leader will be built, incident by incident, crisis by crisis, person by person.

Those who are watching your performance will be looking at a lot of different things as you seek to establish your reputation as a good leader. They want to see that you display personal courage when things get rough. They want to be able to believe you because you have proven your credibility. They want to feel comfortable that you have ample technical expertise in the field of law enforcement and have not forgotten what the job on the street actually entails. They want to know that you can do the job of a cop if called upon. They want to believe that you have patience and persistence – actual staying power – to get the job done when obstacles are thrown in your path.

All of these people need to know that you are willing to take intelligent risks when necessary and that you have the political savvy to navigate your way through the department and the bureaucracy that lies above it. You will be expected, in their minds, to be both a smart risk-taker and a careful risk-manager. These same people want to see you display sound judgment and equally solid decision-making skills. They expect you to show common sense in confronting just about any challenge. Perhaps above all, many of these same people want to know that you will display a caring heart when it comes to dealing with your personnel. From all of these things your diverse observers will construct your reputation.

There may be something perverse in human nature that seemingly makes it easier to construct a bad reputation for someone else than a good one. Be that as it may, by doing the job right and consistently displaying a sense of fair play while sincerely caring about the welfare of your people you will succeed in developing a reputation with the majority of your people that any leader would be proud of. Your reputation truly is everything. By being the leader you know how to be you should never need to worry about your reputation being a positive one.

MENTORING THE NEXT GENERATION OF LEADERS

You owe your organization and your profession more than the best job you can do today. You also are bound to them to help both prepare for the future. You are ethically and morally bound to participate in preparing law enforcement's next generation of leaders. That, too, is a part of your job as a leader.

Succession planning is one of the duties of any quality organization. It is important that the next generation of leaders is prepared to take over as the current leadership moves on over time. This requirement is as true for the law enforcement agency as it is for any other organization, public or private. And it is in preparing this next generation of leaders that you can play an important role.

You have spent a good part of your professional life assembling the education, training and experience that you have used to develop yourself as a successful leader. You have a lot to offer the people who would follow you into a leadership position in your organization. You have a great deal of valuable knowledge and hard-won experience to share. How you go about sharing it is up to you, but there are well-established means, both formal and informal, for doing so.

Whether you are sharing your knowledge and experience in a formal classroom setting or over a cup of coffee, you are serving your organization and your profession well by preparing others to take up where you will one day leave off. You are, in a way, training your replacement. It's one of your responsibilities as an effective leader. You are mentoring the future leaders of your department.

A mentor is sometimes defined as an individual, often older than the individual he is mentoring, who guides the other person's development in his job. Sometimes the mentor is referred to as an advisor or coach. Other times he or she is described as a counselor or guide. Always, the mentor is more experienced in the job (and most likely in life) than is the individual being mentored.

Mentors are not a new thing in the business world. More recently, mentoring has become more prevalent in the fields of education and medicine. Law enforcement in general has been a bit slower to realize the value of a mentoring program, at least in a more formal sense. That doesn't mean that older police leaders have not been providing advice and guidance to their younger colleagues for a long time. They have. But the process is becoming formalized and gaining in popularity as law enforcement's leaders recognize its value.

You may have been taken under the wing of a mentor during your own career development, even if no one thought to apply the term "mentoring" to the process. You probably have learned throughout your career by talking with and questioning those senior to you in the organization. Doubtlessly you have learned a lot in just that way. You have now reached a stage in your career where you should be ready to return the favor by helping those who are equally thirsty for knowledge – the knowledge you already have gathered.

Nothing says you have to wait for a junior leader to come to you asking for assistance. Some of your younger employees may be hesitant to do that. You can instead approach the young man or woman whom you have noticed is particularly sharp, interested and curious, and offer them your assistance in learning the next rung on their career ladder. You don't have to offer to mentor them or even mention the "M word." All you have to do is offer them your help. You may be surprised at how quickly your offer is accepted.

There doesn't have to be anything fancy about your mentoring effort. The key is to be available to answer the questions your "pupil" may pose. But first you have to convince him that you mean it when you say that you want to hear his queries in the first place. That means that you never act like you have no time for him or that his questions are too simple or silly. If you say that you are available to help, be sure you mean it.

Arrange with your mentoree to sit down from time to time to discuss events and issues in both the department and the profession. You may even want to establish a regular schedule. Get his take on personnel situations that may be in progress without betraying confidences he does not need to be privy to. See if he understands the logic behind decisions that have been made. Offer him your insight if he is failing to see the bigger picture or is missing out on the finer points of decision making. Your purpose here is to help him grasp the whole situation where in the past he has only considered his smaller section of it. Your greater purpose is to help him grow. Your goal even beyond that is to aid him in becoming the leader you are today.

There is not an organization on the planet that has too many good leaders. Your job is to help build your own agency's future by preparing its next generation of leaders for the challenges they will soon face. You can (and should) do that as a mentor.

THE COMPLETE PACKAGE

You have put a huge amount of effort into reaching the position that you now hold in your law enforcement agency. You have worked hard to get where you are. You have worked long hours and swallowed some tough shifts. You have sometimes done work that no one else wanted to do. You have successfully carried out some very difficult tasks without complaining. You have been a solid employee and an even better leader. You have "made your bones" and "paid your dues." You are, in a word, "successful."

As a successful leader you owe a few things to the organization that had enough faith in you to put you in your present position. You will continue to lead effectively now while you start preparing the following generation of leaders to take over in the future. You will continue to build on your abilities without resting atop your past accomplishments. You also owe something to your chosen profession. You want to make it better as a consequence of your having been a part of it. You may be able to accomplish that by teaching, writing or mentoring for the betterment of the field. You may be able to do all of these things and more.

But you owe *you*, too. You owe it to yourself and your loved ones never to neglect your own physical and emotional welfare even as you pursue your goal of being an exceptional law enforcement leader. Meanwhile, you owe the truly important people in your life the loyalty and love that they show you in return. In accomplishing that you will vow never to neglect their material and emotional needs as you seek to satisfy your own ego in climbing law enforcement's version of the corporate ladder.

As a leader, then, you are many things. You are a positive role model who leads by example. You are a courageous decision maker who never neglects the teachings of common sense and good judgment in making the difficult calls. You are technically competent in your field without neglecting the human part of the equation. You are firm but fair when it comes to the handling of personnel issues. You put officer safety first in your role as a caring risk manager. You are a unique individual of many parts. The parts make up the complete package that serves you well as a leader.

But your task is not finished just because you are an effective mentor and a successful leader. Every day on the job gives you an additional opportunity to learn more and get better at what you do. Don't miss out on an opportunity to grow. There's always room in the "package" for more experience, more skills, more completely developed abilities. As long as you draw breath the learning process is not complete. You can still be an even better leader.

SUMMARY

You are already an effective leader. You have learned to master your role of leadership and secured a solid grasp on your job's demands. You have figured out how to balance your many tasks and serve as an exceptional role model who leads by example. You are successful because you are an effective communicator in both the spoken and written word.

On your way to becoming an effective leader you have learned how to evaluate employee performance honestly and clearly. You know how to receive and resolve complaints from a variety of sources. You likewise know how to fix it when things go wrong. You excel at mastering the knowledge and skills required to keep your people safe. You can work smoothly with your own boss and handle the news media without losing your cool. You have mastered the in's and out's for surviving the stresses generated by your organization. You have put it all together.

As an exceptional law enforcement leader you will never stop learning your job. You will never cease your quest to get even better at what you do. That's how any organization gets stronger. That's how law enforcement gets better. And that's how you play a key role in getting it all done. That's how you put it all together.

Chapter 15

HOW TO FIGURE OUT WHAT'S NEXT

There can be little doubt that you have had an interesting and rewarding career up to this point. You have seen and done some pretty amazing things. You've learned a lot. Your efforts definitely have benefitted your department and the community you serve. So far, so good. But what's next for you?

There are a lot of cops – particularly those who have enjoyed the success you have in your organization – who are perfectly content to spend the rest of their working life doing just what they are doing. That's perfectly alright. If that is your plan for the future, there is nothing wrong with it – or you. Your employer very much needs your skills and abilities right where they are. You are daily making the world and your organization a better place. But what if that *isn't* your plan? What if you want to do something different? What follows is intended to aid you in exploring the possibilities.

BEING THE BEST

Considering what you do for a living it would not be surprising if you were pretty competitive in the way you look at life and work. You want to be the best. You want to be in charge of the situation. And you want others to see and know you as a leader. Again, there is nothing wrong with that. It helps make you who and what you are. That is a good thing if you want to move into a specialized assignment or attain a higher rank in your agency.

Unless your agency is a very odd one, being the best at what you are doing now will aid you in advancing in the organization. It really is as "simple" as that. Assuming that your agency advances its people primarily based on the basis of demonstrated merit, as it should, doing an excellent job in your present assignment will get you recognized as potentially worthy of the next one. (It won't guarantee that you *get* the position, as there may be other worthy candidates, too.) It will get you noticed, and noticed for the right reasons.

A veteran police supervisor tells the tale of a chronically dissatisfied and loudly disaffected patrol officer assigned to his watch. At every opportunity the woman pointed out to him (and anyone else within hearing distance) the injustices she believed she had suffered at the hands of the department, inasmuch as she had been repeatedly passed over for a specialized assignment. As she put it, "the new kids come in here and get special assignments and us old hands get skipped over, again and again."

The exasperated sergeant expressed his frustration that this employee "just doesn't get it" in spite of his efforts to explain the reason behind her lack of movement in the organization.

"She's lazy. She doesn't do anything she's not absolutely forced to do and she constantly stirs up dissention on the shift. She doesn't do her share of the work and frankly she ticks off just about everyone she comes in contact with," he said. "I've told her and she refuses to get it. She doesn't get a new assignment because she's not doing the one she has now. The department is not going to reward her for not doing her job."

And there lies the crux of the matter. What you know (and what apparently escaped this officer) is that if you want to do something else in your agency you must first prove to your bosses that you are doing an absolutely fantastic job in your current assignment. The "new kids" advanced over this disgruntled officer because they each made a point to excel at being a street cop. They showed themselves to be energetic, hard-working police officers. They were doing on a daily basis what this "entitled" officer did not elect to do.

The same principle applies for you and your place in your own organization. If you want to do something else, do an exceptional job on a consistent basis of what you are doing now. It will be noticed. If you want to be a detective sergeant, do an excellent job as a patrol sergeant. If you want to be a lieutenant, do an incredibly good job of being a sergeant. It works.

People notice when you are striving to do your best. Often they see you as someone who deserves a shot at doing a different, almost certainly more complex job. It may sound corny, but it's true: Doing your best pays off in tangible rewards. Rewards for you.

WHEN TO GO FOR A NEW ASSIGNMENT

When is it time for you to try something new? When do you seek to move from your current assignment or rank to a new one, most likely one with even higher expectations and more responsibilities? An additional question you must answer for yourself is why do you want to do it in the first place? Is it because you are bored or no longer feel challenged in your current posting? Are you being pushed at home to do something with better hours, increased safety and better pay – or all of these things? Is it *really* something that *you* want to do? *Why do you want this change?*

There is nothing wrong with wanting to do something new for any of the preceding reasons. It is perfectly alright (and quite normal) to seek to better your life and that of your loved ones. Making more money, working better hours, being more challenged and perhaps working in a safer environment are all perfectly good reasons for seeking a change in duties. If those are your reasons, that's fine. Just figure out for your own emotional health what those reasons are and be comfortable with them. You don't want to go through a lot of effort and mental agonizing to make the leap and then find out afterwards that you preferred the spot you leapt from.

The queries you will want to answer to your own satisfaction before making the jump include understanding why you want to make the move. You will want to be sure you have the needed support among those at home who are important to you before you ever broach the issue at work. That support will be absolutely critical to a successful transition. Talk with your supervisor about your plans. You may find he or she is anxious to support you. If you sense that the backing isn't there, that may tell you something about your chances. If the support *isn't* forthcoming, try to find out why. You need to know that. You may have some repair work to do.

You'll need to be sure that Big Change is what you really want for yourself, too. Life is too short to spend a big portion of it in a new assignment that you really didn't want. You also should be comfortable that you have the requisite knowledge, skills and abilities to succeed in your new role. If your honest assessment tells that you fall short in some key area, you must establish a plan and a timetable for obtaining those things. It may slow your progress a bit, but you will have the added satisfaction once you get there of knowing that you are adequately equipped to do well.

Do start the wheels in motion to seek a new assignment when you sense that you have become bored or burnt out (or are becoming so) in your current one. Do it when you sense that your interests or focus have changed. Perhaps you have always felt great satisfaction in your excellent reputation as a savvy street sergeant. But now you find yourself more and more interested in the challenges of detective supervisor. That's alright. Go for it if you have all the pieces in place.

Do it when it feels right for everyone concerned, including yourself. But there's an exception to that rule that may nonetheless benefit your career plans down the road. For the future benefits it may bring you, consider accepting an assignment that will help your organization even when it is not something you are terribly excited about doing for yourself. A successful police chief tells a story about being tabbed for an assignment as juvenile team sergeant when all he wanted to do was continue enjoying his role as a night watch patrol supervisor. His boss called him when he was on vacation to tell him of his new reporting station. He was more than a little angry about what he considered underhand maneuverings. But he swallowed his misgivings and swore to make the best of his new assignment because his department felt his skills were needed in the new spot. He placed his needs subservient to those of his organization. He later felt that his decision contributed heavily to his rapid rise through the ranks of the department. That may not happen for you, but it certainly could. Sacrifices now have been known to pay off big time later.

Go for a new assignment when you have conferred with your significant others and your boss and you have determined that you have the support you need across the board. Next, determine that your resume meets the expectations of the new assignment or position. Then, be prepared to invest the time, energy and emotion to go all out in winning the position you desire.

If, on the other hand, you conclude after careful analysis that it isn't the time to go for a big life and work change, be comfortable in continuing in your current job status. Continue to seek the satisfaction that comes from knowing you have contributed and have done a job well. Know that your employer, your profession and your community have benefitted from what you are doing and will continue to do so. Take satisfaction from your successes. Meanwhile, keep preparing for the change that well may occur down the road. Get even better at your current assignment in order to be ready for the next one. Get additional, relevant education and training if you find you need it. It will help you to be ready when it is clearly time to go for a new assignment.

IS PROMOTION FOR YOU?

What if the new assignment you have in mind is promotion? In that case, many of the same questions and considerations noted previously still apply. Once again you should check with your loved ones to assure that they are willing to take on the additional challenges that go along with the increased benefits. Everyone involved should be aware that the investment of additional time and energy will be required. You'll need to get your boss's input, as well. Does he feel you are ready? Is he willing to help you prepare and proceed? If you sense any hesitancy to support you on the part of your supervisor you should explore further. Ask him to explain his concerns, if he has not done so. In most organizations a lack of support from a promotional candidate's supervisor will make it unlikely that the competitor will succeed in his advancement efforts, at least for the time being.

Be sure you have decided to go for promotion for the right reasons, which certainly will include all the benefits the change potentially could bring for you and yours. A "wrong" reason would be to anticipate facing *fewer* responsibilities or challenges, which will almost never turn out to be the case in the real world. Promotion doesn't work that way.

Be equally certain before you put your name in the promotional hat that you are willing and able to do the necessary preparatory work that precedes a successful promotional effort. You will need to set aside time – perhaps a good deal of it – for study. If your life's other priorities do not permit that time and energy investment just now, this probably isn't the time to grab for the brass ring. Your run for the prize may need to wait until you have other obligations under control. Don't bite off more than you can chew and strangle because you had too many competing priorities.

Achieving promotion likely will mean leaving your comfort zone, an area of expertise or responsibility that you know you have mastered. There will be new, sometimes unfamiliar challenges following promotion to a higher rank. You will be expected to master them. Certainly doing so is something you can do or learn to do. But it likely will require you to learn, polish or apply some new skills. You undoubtedly will be *able* to meet the challenge. Just be certain that you are *willing* to do it.

It is equally important that you are willing to spend the necessary time, effort and money to obtain the required, additional education or training if you do not yet have the needed paper qualifications for the rank you are seeking. Many law enforcement organizations require college training for advanced rank positions. Going back to school (if you are not there already) can be an effort for those who have been out of the classroom a while and now have a family to balance with work while simultaneously hitting the books. Be comfortable that you have the time and energy to carry all of these tasks while remaining physically and emotionally healthy. If you find that it isn't wise to do all of that just now rest assured that a better time likely will come a little later.

Finally, remain aware throughout your decision-making process that things will change in your life following promotion, whether you are taking on your first supervisory assignment or moving from one leadership post to a higher one. Your employees' relations with you will be altered to at least some extent. You may find that you have fewer truly close friends. (The good news is that you likely will make some new ones.) Your personal attitude and responsibilities towards your organization will change, as well. You will be expected to support the decisions of the agency's leadership once those decisions have been made, whether or not you personally agree with them. The higher in the organization you go, the more you will be expected to see and grasp the big picture that exists beyond your own area of responsibility. You will be expected to be a team player, not a grandstander who works only for his own recognition. Your organization will expect a lot. You know that and you know that the right answer is "I can do it." Just be sure that you really mean it.

Also be sure that you really want to be promoted. It's hard to go back once you've made the jump. Certainly, you can request demotion and some really good cops have done that. Just know that it will be hard to go forward in the future if you change your mind about advancement later. You can do it and others have. But you'll have some tough questions to answer first.

Be prepared to not succeed your first time at bat. Most don't. You'll be disappointed, but you can learn from the experience in order to be a stronger competitor the next time. Ask those who tested you how you can do better. With a positive attitude and good preparation you *will* get there.

Promotion isn't for everyone. Doubtlessly you are doing an excellent job right where you are. But once you have determined that promotion is for you, go for it with all you've got. Expect to succeed. Do what's required. Then, enjoy the fruits of all your labors. You and your organization will be the better off for your hard work.

WHAT'S YOUR CAREER PLAN?

Perhaps your goal is a specialized assignment. Maybe it's promotion to a higher rank. Could be it is to stay with the assignment you are now enjoying with the goal of retiring in five years. Whatever is in the crosshairs for you, it is smart to make plans for getting there right now. It's later than you think.

In making your plans you should take into account how much more time you intend to spend working and adjust your career plans accordingly. If you have five years left on the calendar and you are currently a sergeant it may be unrealistic to expect that you will become chief of a large police department. (A smaller one may certainly be within your reach.) It is alright to overreach a little in your planning, but be realistic in your expectations to avoid unnecessary disappointments.

Know, too, that you will need to have the requisite education and training for what you want to do tomorrow. In some cases experience may substitute for formal schooling. Size up what you think you want to do well in advance so you will have what's required to get in the door once the time comes. Do your homework and you will increase your chances of getting what you want.

As you plan for what you want to do once police work is in your rearview mirror you'll need to answer some basic questions. What is your dream life after retirement? Do you want to work or relax, or do a little of both? Do you intend to relocate, or are you willing to? Is your ego ready to let you do a less-demanding, but less-prestigious job? Can you work for a lot less money? Once again determine in advance how those who are important in your life figure into your plans. Will you have their support for what you really itch to do? You may want to have a Plan B in your back pocket.

You already know that you will need to stay active in order to protect both your physical and mental health. You know that cops who have dropped overnight from 80 to zero and planted their rear-end in a lounger oftentimes don't live long. You don't want that to happen to you. But also realize that not everyone can retire to become a "consultant." The world simply does not have a need for *that* many law enforcement experts. You may have to get a little more imaginative in your planning efforts.

The very good news is that people are living longer, healthier lives today. You may well have time for multiple careers before you are ready for a rocking chair in front of the fireplace. You have done a lot for society and you have a great deal more to offer. Give some thought now as to how you want to spend the rest of your life. Your loved ones, your organization and you will benefit from it. Keep giving. You surely will receive much in return.

SUMMARY

For you career planning begins today and continues for the rest of the time that you work for a living. Your targets and goals may change over time, but your planning for what comes next should never stop. Some hard work will be required, but you are used to that. Continuing education may also be in your future, but you should be willing to take on that challenge, as well. There is little, including becoming the CEO of a law enforcement agency, that should be beyond your reach if you want it badly enough and are willing to do the work required to get there.

You will meet challenges en route to attaining your ultimate goals. There well may be temporary diversions and delays in your journey. Those are nothing new to you, however, and in spite of them you will continue to reach for the next rung on the ladder. Adversity can slow but not stop your journey. Never underestimate your own inner strengths and abilities as you steadily advance your career.

At the same time you should realize that there is absolutely nothing wrong with staying in the assignment you are in, if your department will permit it, and continue to get better and better at what you do. If you are a sergeant, every law enforcement agency in America needs more excellent first-line supervisors. Seek to be the absolute best you can be and your organization will thank you. Likewise, every policing organization in the country is constantly in search of additional, highly competent mid-managers. If you happen to be a skilled lieutenant or commander and choose to remain in that enviable position, more power to you. Concentrate on getting even more skilled at what you do. Law enforcement needs you right where you are.

The same holds true if you are a leader in a specialized or technical area of law enforcement. Your expertise and leadership are desperately needed by your employer. Stick with what you enjoy for as long as you enjoy it and your organization will allow you to remain there. It's likely that what you are doing now will be of continuing and great use to your organization. In other words, it's alright NOT to want to move up in rank if you are content in what you are doing and feel that you will remain that way. It would be ill-advised to seek a job that you're not sure you would enjoy or prosper in doing.

In the end it is up to YOU to plan the remainder of your leadership career. No one can (or should) do it for you. You have the skills. You have the knowledge and you have the talent. The path ahead is for your choosing.

INDEX

Time, 74
Toolbox, 50
Touches, personal, 12
Trainer, 29–30, 116
Training, 7, 25, 111, 175, 177
Training, firearms, 110
Training, safety, 29
Traits, 43
Traits, personality, 28
Transition, 173
Trust, mutual, 147
Truth, 19, 85, 140
Truthfulness, 43

U

Understanding, 61
United Way, 33
Upstaging, 143
Use of force, 32

V

Venting, 77
Views, 20
Violence, 32
Vision, 50
Volunteering, 144

W

Warning, 126
Weaknesses, 76
Weapon retention, 115
Whining, 11
Words, 66
Work, 141
Writer, 67
Writing, 64
Wrongdoing, 85–86